May–August 2017

Day by Day
with
God

Rooting women's lives in the Bible

The Bible Reading Fellowship
Christina Press
Abingdon/Tunbridge Wells

The Bible Reading Fellowship
15 The Chambers, Vineyard
Abingdon OX14 3FE
brf.org.uk

The Bible Reading Fellowship (BRF) is a Registered Charity (233280)

ISBN 978 0 85746 446 0

Distributed in Australia by:
MediaCom Education Inc, PO Box 610, Unley, SA 5061
Tel: 1 800 811 311 | admin@mediacom.org.au

Distributed in New Zealand by:
Scripture Union Wholesale, PO Box 760, Wellington
Tel: 04 385 0421 | suwholesale@clear.net.nz

Acknowledgements
Scripture quotations taken from The Holy Bible, New International Version (Anglicised edition), copyright © 1979, 1984, 2011 by Biblica. Used by permission of Hodder & Stoughton Publishers, an Hachette UK company. All rights reserved. 'NIV' is a registered trademark of Biblica. UK trademark number 1448790.

Scripture quotations from THE MESSAGE. Copyright © by Eugene H. Peterson 1993, 1994, 1995. Used by permission of NavPress Publishing Group.

Scripture quotations taken from the Holy Bible, New Living Translation, copyright © 1996, 2004, 2007, 2013. Used by permission of Tyndale House Publishers, Inc., Carol Stream, Illinois 60188. All rights reserved.

Scripture quotations taken from the Holy Bible, English Standard Version, published by HarperCollins Publishers, © 2001 Crossway Bibles, a division of Good News Publishers. Used by permission. All rights reserved.

Extracts from the Authorised Version of the Bible (The King James Bible), the rights in which are vested in the Crown, are reproduced by permission of the Crown's Patentee, Cambridge University Press.

Scripture taken from the Holy Bible, New International Reader's Version®. Copyright © 1996, 1998, Biblica. All rights reserved throughout the world. Used by permission of Biblica.

Scripture quotations taken from The New Revised Standard Version of the Bible, Anglicised Edition, copyright © 1989, 1995 by the Division of Christian Education of the National Council of the Churches of Christ in the USA, are used by permission. All rights reserved.

Printed by Gutenberg Press, Tarxien, Malta

Contents

Writers in this issue

Jennifer Rees Larcombe runs Beauty from Ashes, an organisation that supports people adjusting to bereavement and trauma

Alison Teale works as an administrator in tertiary education and has worked as a freelance writer and translator for 20 years.

Rosemary Green has four adult offspring and 14 grandchildren. She and her husband live in Abingdon, where she is involved mainly in ministry among Seniors in her local church.

Henrietta Blyth is a member of St Mary's, Bryanston Square, and a keen gardener, despite living in north-west London. She loves knitting and helping people to become who God created them to be. She works as the CEO of Inter-Health Worldwide, an international health charity.

Helen Williams has worked in music, education, management consultancy and administration, but today finds herself working mostly alongside her husband, an Anglican bishop, in all sorts of contexts. Since writing the notes in this issue, she intends to devote her time to her friends!

Amy Boucher Pye is a writer and speaker who lives in north London. She runs the *Woman Alive* book club and has written *Finding Myself in Britain* (Authentic, 2015) and *The Living Cross* (BRF, 2016). She blogs at amyboucherpye.com.

Bola Adamolekun is a huge fan of dark chocolate, speculative fiction and old buildings. She loves dancing with friends, trying to play badminton competitively and visiting her local library as often as she can. She is a writer and a potter. She is also a pioneer priest with the Church of England.

Bridget Plass trained as an actress and has also worked as a secondary school teacher, residential social worker and a facilitator of women's groups. With her husband Adrian she performs as a speaker and entertainer, and she has written three books for BRF. Bridget and Adrian have four children.

Ann Warren began her career in the BBC as a producer and scriptwriter, subsequently training as a pastoral counsellor and life coach. She was a regular Christian Viewpoint speaker and has written a number of books, including her personal story of healing, *No Place to Belong*.

Sandra Wheatley remains as active as possible despite the constraints of MS and a wheelchair. She enjoys an extensive prayer ministry and has mastered swimming and praying at the same time.

Ali Herbert and Jill Rattle write...

Can you remember a time when you suddenly knew you were a grown-up? Perhaps you were looking over your shoulder, waiting for an adult to arrive and take charge, and realised they weren't coming—because the adult was you. Jill remembers an occasion having a drink with friends: one was involved in appointing a vice-chancellor, another in appointing a bishop and a third in selecting naval officers, and she thought to herself, 'Oh, goodness, we really are the grown-ups now!'

Being a grown-up brings responsibilities and the need for wisdom to fulfil them. We sometimes call that wisdom 'maturity'. But what is the difference between ordinary personal or physical maturity and 'Christian' maturity? All Christians are called to spiritual maturity, and so this edition begins with Jennifer Rees Larcombe beautifully exploring what that means for us and how to reach it.

The theme of 'wisdom' or 'spiritual maturity' occurs again and again in our readings, whether they're about Joseph on his personal road from immaturity to wisdom through hard experience, or the fruits and gifts of the Spirit that mark the mature Christian, or the ageless wisdom of Solomon in his Proverbs.

We welcome a new writer, Helen Williams, who looks at the characteristics of mature friendship and challenges us to deepen our relationships with one another and with God. We also think through some of the worries that assail us as adults and how to deal with them. We face the high standards that Jesus sets us in the Beatitudes and chew over the 'meat of the word' found in Paul's letter to the Romans: no 'baby milk' there!

Finally we stand on some of the holiest ground in scripture and listen in on Jesus' amazing high-priestly prayer to his Father and his yearning for us all to be one with God, Father, Son and Holy Spirit. What a privilege!

We pray that all of us, through these readings, will grow up a little more into spiritual maturity, to reflect better the life of Jesus in the power of the Spirit to the glory of God.

Ali Herbert and Jill Rattle

Christian maturity

Jennifer Rees Larcombe writes:

We were all in our late teens, squashed together in the church lounge for the last night of a youth mission which had been led by a group of enthusiastic undergraduates. Most of us had either received Christ for the first time or committed our entire lives to him. 'This evening,' said the most handsome of the students, 'I've asked my father to speak.' Disappointment was tangible as a very old man stood up (although anyone over 40 would have looked ancient to us). 'I hear you've had a wonderful week,' he began as we beamed our hearty agreement. 'I guess there's about a hundred of you in here. All baby Christians, but, sadly, very few of you will grow up to maturity. In five years' time, when you're out there in the world, only about 60 of you will have maintained your enthusiasm for Christ. Twenty years from now, only 20 of you will have managed to withstand the pressures of work, child-rearing and the worries and disappointments of life. In 30 years, you may still be churchgoers, but Christ will be a very small part of your life. Forty years from now, only two of you will still remain completely devoted to him and enthusiastically serving his people.'

I'm not sure if the old guy's statistics were correct but I will never forget the way his face shone as he explained, from Colossians 2:6–7, what it means to become a mature Christian. 'So then, just as you received Christ Jesus as Lord, continue to live your lives in him, rooted and built up in him, strengthened in the faith… and overflowing with thankfulness' (NIV).

All of us, reading this, probably hope to become spiritually mature, but how is this possible in our busy lives today? Over the next six days we shall explore some ideas.

Growing up backwards

**God, I'm not trying to rule the roost… I've cultivated a quiet heart.
Like a baby content in its mother's arms, my soul is a baby content.**
(*THE MESSAGE*)

Psalm 131 was written by one of the most successful soldiers and states-men who ever lived—but David had also learnt the secret of spiritual maturity.

I felt overwhelmed by responsibility as I looked down at my first baby, lying helpless in my arms, totally dependent on me for everything. It would take years of feeding problems, potty training and help with homework to transform her into an independent, self-sufficient, mature woman. Successful parenting means producing an adult who can live perfectly well without you. God, however, has a totally opposite view of parenting; in fact, I think he brings his children up backwards.

When a mature adult becomes a baby Christian, God has to gradually break down her carefully acquired self-dependence to the point where she relies on him completely. This is not because he is some kind of power-hungry tyrant; he simply knows that our lives are safe and satisfy-ing only when we allow him to be completely in control.

The more successful we have been at running our own lives, the harder it is to take on board Jesus' words that we must become as dependent and trusting as little children (Matthew 18:3). Paul goes even further when he reminds us that 'in him we live and move and have our being' (Acts 17:28, NIV): we need to be as utterly dependent as a baby in the womb.

Some Christians take a whole lifetime to attain maturity, while others develop much faster. We will be exploring some of the reasons for that, but I suspect that, for many of us, growth is speeded by adversity. God never sends our disasters; he simply uses them to reveal how unable we are to control the events of our lives, and how able he is to help us, what-ever loss or disappointment we face.

Looking back, Lord, I can see how close you've always been in my bad times, even if I couldn't feel your presence. I can also see how amazingly you have brought good out of those difficult situations. Thank you, Lord.

JENNIFER REES LARCOMBE

A mature Christian knows she's loved

I pray that you, being rooted and established in love, may have power… to grasp how wide and long and high and deep is the love of Christ… that you may be filled to the measure of all the fullness of God. (NIV)

Paul shows us that Christian maturity is based on a love relationship. It has nothing to do with age, gifts or how long we have been a church member. Too many churches are strangled by people who, because of their age, feel they have earned the right to control everything—but have long since 'lost their first love' (see Revelation 2:4).

My mother told me, 'When you grow up you'll meet many people who know lots about God or do great things for him, but you'll only meet a few who just want to be close to him and love him for himself alone—not what they can get out of him.'

Sadly, many of us are actually afraid of getting close to God because we have a false view of what he is like. We develop our picture of him mostly from the way our parents treated us. If they were critical, harsh, absent or disinterested, we might think God is the same.

If our parents were over-indulgent, we could expect God to be a per-petual 'Father Christmas', ready to grant our every wish. In that case, it may be resentment, not fear, that inhibits intimacy, because whenever God fails to answer our prayers as we want, we throw a tantrum. We have not yet discovered that God always knows exactly what is best for us. Part of our maturing process is about learning to see God as the Bible portrays him.

If we never felt loved by our parents, it is more of a battle to grasp the unfathomable depth of his unconditional love for each of us individually, or how greatly he longs for our love in return. However, it is definitely a battle we can win—with God's help.

Lord, in the hard times, I'm sometimes tempted to believe you can't love me, or even that you're powerless. Help me cling to the solid fact that you are all-powerful and you love me everlastingly and unconditionally.

JENNIFER REES LARCOMBE

A mature Christian puts God first

'The seeds that fell among the thorns represent those who hear the message, but all too quickly the message is crowded out by the cares and riches and pleasures of this life. And so they never grow into maturity.' (NLT)

Reading this verse, we might think, 'Cares and worries are inevitable, being rich isn't wrong, and surely God isn't against pleasure?' (see 1 Timothy 6:17). So why does Jesus say that these things impede Christian maturity? Perhaps by 'cares' he means the kind of pressure and tension we experience when we are striving to meet our own self-made goals. For example, we might think, 'I'll only feel secure if I make lots of money or get to the top at work', 'I'm only worth anything if I look gorgeous and have a perfect home', or 'I must find a man because I can't cope alone.' Using all our energy to achieve goals like these can lead to crippling stress or disappointment.

Jesus is not saying that riches are wrong; many rich Christians see their wealth as a God-given way to expand his kingdom. God loves to see us enjoying the pleasures he gives us, but when they become all-important they cause our spiritual lives to be 'choked' (v. 7). Kristy and Tim were enthusiastic Christians, working hard in their church, but once they started a family the pleasures (and pressures) of being a perfect housewife and mother soon took first place in Kristy's life, while Tim became passionate about gardening and DIY. They both became 'too busy' for church.

In verse 13 Jesus says that some of us fail to reach maturity because of temptation. Fortunately he doesn't say that maturity means never giving way to temptation. Obviously we do our best to please the Lord by avoiding things he forbids, but we are still human—so we sin. Perhaps maturity develops when we fully understand what Jesus did by dying on the cross, and realise that a mature Christian isn't perfect—just forgiven often.

Lord Jesus, I'm sorry that I so often indulge in that sin I dismiss, so lightly, as 'my little weakness'. Help me to appreciate what the cross cost you. I so long to please you in everything I do and avoid doing.

JENNIFER REES LARCOMBE

A mature Christian loves her Bible

'The word of the Lord endures for ever.' And this is the word that was preached to you… Therefore… like newborn babies, crave pure spiritual milk, so that by it you may grow up in your salvation. (NIV)

There seems to be one thing that is common to all mature Christians: they have developed the habit of giving God their undivided attention for a few minutes every day—to talk and listen to him. There are many ways of hearing his voice. Perhaps the most popular is through reading the Bible, not as a historical document but as a personal love letter, speaking right into their lives to give them wisdom and strength for the coming day.

This is the living 'word' that Peter tells us we should crave, like hungry babies. He does not mean we should simply stay with the nice, comforting passages; we also need to take seriously the more challenging ones. Jesus said that we show him our love by obeying his words (John 14:15), and a mature Christian obeys very quickly when she senses the Lord asking her to do something or stop doing it. 'Don't fool yourself into thinking that you are a listener when you are…letting the Word go in one ear and out the other', says James 1:22 (*THE MESSAGE*).

We have probably all had the disillusioning experience of thinking we heard God speak and dashing off to do something rash—only to discover we were mistaken. Perhaps part of maturity is learning to recognise God's voice, as well as acquiring the humility to check his words out with a wise friend.

One of the hallmarks of an immature Christian is to use prayer as a way of getting God to do what we want rather than discovering what God wants to do and asking him how we can best cooperate. As we mature in our relationship with him, prayer becomes less about 'asking' and more about listening, less about words and more about comfortable, companionable silence.

Perhaps you need this prayer: Lord, you don't seem to speak to me through the Bible like you once did. Recently it has felt dry and dull. Please revive my hunger for your word and restore my ability to hear you.

JENNIFER REES LARCOMBE

A mature Christian looks like Jesus

So Christ himself gave… pastors and teachers, to equip his people for works of service, so that the body of Christ may be built up until we all reach unity in the faith… and become mature, attaining to the whole measure of the fullness of Christ. (NIV)

Have you ever thought, 'I could be such a great Christian if only I lived alone on a desert island'? While Christ loves each of us individually and values, above all else, our private relationship with himself, he also sees us collectively, closely interwoven with each other, functioning as his body here on earth.

In today's passage Paul tells us that we develop maturity through unity as we serve Christ with others. So, nice as that island may sound, we need to be part of our local church. It is as we share our lives with other people that we develop the 'fruit of the Spirit' (Galatians 5:22–23). These are simply the qualities of Jesus that God wants us all to imitate as we gradually grow more like his Son (Romans 8:29). Other Christians can be maddeningly irritating, can't they? Yet how else are we going to develop the fruits of patience, gentleness and self-control than by interacting with them?

Paul also reminds us that we need leaders to pastor and teach us. The fruit of faithfulness develops rapidly when we do not always agree with our leaders. Christians who hop frequently from one church to the next, hunting for excitement, seem to stay immature until they settle down and begin loving other people sacrificially. Jesus constantly encountered difficult religious leaders and fellow believers, yet he forgave them, accepted their failings and limitations and kept on loving them.

All the same, when Jesus encountered leaders who were abusing their roles destructively, he wasn't afraid to speak out—before moving on to minister somewhere else. He may guide us to do the same if the church we attend is seriously impeding our growth. However, we will never grow to maturity anywhere else until we have totally forgiven the people who hurt us in our previous church.

Lord, help me remember that you live in each of the people at church, just as you live in me. Help me to realise that you come to me in them, and you want to reach them through me.

JENNIFER REES LARCOMBE

11

A mature Christian keeps growing

I want to know Christ… becoming like him… Not that I have already… arrived at my goal, but I press on to take hold of that for which Christ Jesus took hold of me. (NIV)

Paul must have helped millions of people to grow up spiritually. Interestingly, though, his own goal was not spiritual maturity—at least, not after he became a Christian. As a Pharisee (vv. 5–6), Paul strove to achieve perfection through keeping God's rules, but after meeting Jesus he threw that goal away as mere rubbish (v. 8). All he wanted to do was to know Christ and be like him.

Paul must have loved talking to the people who had met Jesus before the crucifixion—heard him speak, lived with him and watched the way he behaved on the day when he died. Yet Paul soon realised that the Holy Spirit makes it possible for us to know Jesus in an even more intimate way than they had, because we not only live 'with' him but we also live 'in' him (v. 9) and he lives in us (Galatians 3:27).

This is the closest relationship that any of us can ever have, and Paul equates maturity with the desire for it (v. 15). Yet he makes it clear in the previous two verses that he has not yet achieved that level of intimacy himself. He is constantly hungry for more of Jesus.

Perhaps that kind of yearning, along with humility, is also a hallmark of maturity. I have often observed that new Christians are so excited about their faith that they can give the impression they 'know it all', but the further we grow towards maturity, the more conscious we are of the sins that hold us back from Jesus and how much we still have to learn about him.

We sing several songs at church that feature the phrase 'I'm desperate for you'. Immaturity says, 'I'm desperate for your power, healing and financial provision', while maturity says, 'I'm desperate for you alone, your friendship and presence as I serve you with everything I have.'

Lord, sometimes I'm definitely not desperate for you—particularly when you do things I don't like, or when I enjoy doing things you don't like. Please refresh my desperation, and keep it burning in my heart.

JENNIFER REES LARCOMBE

The life of Joseph

Alison Teale writes:

Over the next two weeks we will be looking at some incidents from the life of Joseph—owner of the coat of many colours, who dreamed dreams, was a tad too haughty for his own good, was sold into slavery in Egypt by his brothers, rose to be Pharaoh's right-hand man and was well positioned to save the people of his extended family from a seven-year famine.

Many people have drawn valuable lessons from the overarching span of Joseph's 110 years of life. They include the fact that God is ultimately in charge, that he can use the bad things that happen to us for our good and the good of others, that our life path doesn't always follow the route we think it ought, and that exercising forgiveness and mercy are necessary qualities of those who seek to serve God. However, in looking for the big themes, we often overlook day-to-day dilemmas, traumas and concerns. One short sentence of text can conceal a gamut of emotions and condense a difficult or painful decision into a perfunctory statement of fact. What is actually going on when we read, 'His brothers pulled Joseph up out of the cistern and sold him for twenty shekels of silver to the Ishmaelites, who took him to Egypt' (Genesis 37:28)? Did Joseph stand there and acquiesce? If not, why did no one listen to him and have second thoughts? Were the brothers in control of their actions or were they full of wine and unthinking of the consequences—or were they cold and calculating? Where was the one brother who hoped to save Joseph, at the exact time when he was needed? Why was he not eating with the others?

So then, rather than repeating familiar lessons, I have taken verses from the earlier part of Joseph's life and tried to get behind the text, asking questions that are not usually asked in our focus on the 'big story'. I hope these readings will help you look at a familiar story in a new light and encourage you that God is there in the little things, the everyday joys and struggles, even when we feel he is remote and far away. Then, when you stand back and look at your 'big story', you may be able to see the overarching pattern of his involvement in your life.

A word in season

[Jacob said] 'Will your mother and I and your brothers actually come and bow down to the ground before you?' His brothers were jealous of him, but his father kept the matter in mind. (NIV)

Managing a large family is full of challenges. I have four children and know what it is like to try to treat them fairly, making sure they all get the same attention, food, gifts and opportunities. I managed to keep things fair for a few years, but life gets more complicated as children grow older and begin to develop their own interests and aspirations. Their material needs vary greatly, being 'fair' becomes a trade-off, and a tension develops between helping them each to cultivate a sense of self-worth and teaching them that modesty is also of value!

I wonder if Jacob was mistaken to give Jacob such an elaborately woven garment (v. 3). I don't know why he did it. The coat was bound to make his brothers jealous, and it probably contributed to Joseph's precocious sense of self-importance, which prompted him to share his dreams with his brothers and father.

We will never know the context in which Joseph spoke out, but even words spoken casually in conversation over a meal can have a powerful effect. Jacob's reply (in the verse quoted above) appears to be an attempt to calm the situation, but, like most parents in such a situation, he kept his child's words at the back of his mind. It is possible that Joseph would have had the dreams even without owning the coat, but did the owning of the coat predispose him to such thoughts? We may never know.

For me, the lesson is to take care how we treat our children or grandchildren in relation to each other, and to take care over the words we speak. We need wisdom to know when to share what we feel God has put on our hearts, or whether it is wise to share it at all.

'May these words of my mouth and this meditation of my heart be pleasing in your sight, Lord, my Rock and my Redeemer' (Psalm 19:14).

ALISON TEALE

Don't just stand there...

So when the Midianite merchants came by, his brothers pulled Joseph up out of the cistern and sold him for twenty shekels of silver to the Ishmaelites, who took him to Egypt. (NIV)

The story of Joseph being sold into slavery in Egypt by his jealous brothers was told to me at Sunday school in a way that airbrushed the brutal reality of the situation and made me think it was an acceptable occurrence. Of course, it was not. Even if the act is depicted as an essential part of God's bigger plan to save Joseph's family several decades later, it should not detract from the fact that what these brothers did to their younger sibling was an unjustifiable crime—attempted murder followed by trafficking a young person to a foreign country with no recourse to help.

Think yourself into Joseph's situation. Empty cisterns are deep. There is no way out. If he had been left there, he would have died of thirst. He begged for his life while his brothers feasted (Genesis 42:21). Yet where was Reuben when the slave traders passed by? He was the brother who had been planning to rescue Joseph from the cistern, but he was notably absent, or silent, at the moment of sale. Right then, I don't think Joseph would have been comforted by being told of God's promise to Abraham that his descendants would be liberated from oppression in Egypt, or that his suffering would play a key role in getting them to Egypt in the first place (Genesis 15:13–14).

Those of us who have lived long and suffered various tragedies can probably look back and see how God has woven his purpose through those events, but at the time they were agony. Let's be careful not to trot out well-worn platitudes to those who are hurting, but, rather, learn to identify with their present pain and support them through it until the bigger picture eventually comes into focus.

'Continue to remember those in prison as if you were together with them in prison, and those who are ill-treated as if you yourselves were suffering' (Hebrews 13:3).

ALISON TEALE

Seek God and work wholeheartedly

The Lord was with Joseph so that he prospered, and he lived in the house of his Egyptian master. When his master saw that the Lord was with him and that the Lord gave him success in everything he did, Joseph found favour in his eyes. (NIV)

God prospered Joseph while he was living and working in Potiphar's house. The Hebrew word for 'Egypt' is similar to the word for 'a narrow or restricted place', so we could think of this as God blessing Joseph when his circumstances were tight. Although we believe in grace (God giving us richly what we do not deserve), there is still a dynamic in the kingdom of God in which God prospers those who follow his commands and work wholeheartedly. Although life had dealt Joseph a rough deal, he chose not to wallow in self-pity or be dishonest and lazy while planning to escape; instead he chose to seek God and work wholeheartedly.

I don't think that God necessarily prospered Joseph in monetary terms; rather, God enabled him to master and succeed at the tasks he was allocated, so that he honoured his master as well as earning God's blessing. When we are in tight circumstances, it can be a challenge to stick to the straight and narrow.

As I write these notes, I am in the process of relocating, finding a new home and looking for a new job. It is exciting but it is also scary, and money is tight. I got a job interview and needed a new suit, so I bought one. The interview was successful and I was offered the job, but do you know how tempting it was to loop the price labels back on to that suit and return it for a refund? Very tempting, because the suit had cost a week's housekeeping. I struggled but I did not fall for the temptation, because I believe that God won't prosper my relocation if I don't honour him. We all have moments when we're tempted not to be wholehearted. Ask God for the strength to stand firm.

Lord, in everything I undertake, help me to seek you in obedience and to work wholeheartedly, doing what is good and right and faithful before you. Amen

ALISON TEALE

A lesser of two evils

When [Joseph's] master heard the story his wife told him, saying, 'This is how your slave treated me,' he burned with anger. Joseph's master took him and put him in prison, the place where the king's prisoners were confined. (NIV)

A key event in Joseph's life was the moment when Potiphar's wife made a sexual advance towards him and he rebuffed it, fleeing from her but leaving his outer garment clutched in her hands. Adultery was a crime punishable by death and it is possible that Potiphar's wife cried rape in order to protect herself from accusation. Potiphar was angry and Joseph was imprisoned, but the text does not tell us at whom Potiphar's anger was directed. We assume it must have been at Joseph, but we could be wrong.

Some commentators believe that Potiphar, being captain of the guard, was also Pharaoh's executioner, with the power to dispense justice on the spot. If that was the case, why was Joseph not executed directly? Perhaps Potiphar knew that his wife had a restless streak and that there was more to the incident than met the eye. He had also come to know that Joseph was a good and faithful manager and that the crime he was accused of was out of character. Potiphar's anger may thus have been directed at his wife, caused by the thought of losing a good slave.

Interestingly, we do not hear Joseph say anything in his own defence. If he had spoken and his words had been believed, Potiphar's wife would have been put to death, with shame brought on the household. By imprisoning Joseph, albeit unjustly, Potiphar spared not only Joseph's life but also the life of his feckless wife, although he lost a valuable worker in the process.

How easy it is to rush into a situation and assume the 'obvious'. Like Potiphar, we need wisdom and insight to understand what is really happening in a difficult situation and how to resolve it so that good can come from it.

'Indeed, I was born guilty, a sinner when my mother conceived me. You desire truth in the inward being; therefore teach me wisdom in my secret heart' (Psalm 51:5–6, NRSV).

ALISON TEALE

A strange kind of promotion

The warder put Joseph in charge of all those held in the prison, and he was made responsible for all that was done there. The warder paid no attention to anything under Joseph's care, because the Lord was with Joseph and gave him success in whatever he did. (NIV)

I have no idea what a prison was like in ancient Egypt, but whatever is meant by 'dungeon', Joseph would have found himself in a place where he would rather not be, especially as he had been put there unjustly, albeit as an act of mercy to save him from execution.

Nevertheless, this apparent setback proved to be the opposite. Maybe Joseph's reputation had gone before him, or perhaps the prison warden had been a guest at Potiphar's house and witnessed Joseph's capabilities. Possibly, Potiphar had had a word in the warden's ear. Whatever the reason, Joseph soon found himself in a position of responsibility. Effectively he went from running Potiphar's household to running Pharaoh's prison. Although we could think of running a prison as a demotion, it could be seen as a promotion for Joseph. The prison would have been much larger than Potiphar's house in terms of area and the number of people it housed, so he would have greater responsibility there. Think of the rotas, the management of provisions and the maintenance schedules he would have had to oversee—and the people problems he would have had to resolve. Of course, he was still a prisoner himself, but being a prisoner was probably not much different from being a slave: either way, he was not a free man.

I find it encouraging that Joseph was able to use his gifts to great effect in very challenging and unexpected circumstances, and that God enabled him to succeed. Sometimes life takes a difficult turn that we do not expect, but it is good to think that we can use our God-given abilities to maximum effect even in a situation that, on the surface, looks like a setback.

Lord God, help me to look beyond the surface of my situation and see how I can bring the gifts you have given me to bear in what I do.

ALISON TEALE

A friend in need

Joseph said to [the cupbearer] '… When all goes well with you, remember me and show me kindness; mention me to Pharaoh and get me out of this prison. I was forcibly carried off from the land of the Hebrews, and even here I have done nothing to deserve being put in a dungeon.' (NIV)

Can you recall someone who has done something kind for you? Having been a clergy wife for three decades, I can remember people being more kind to me than perhaps they otherwise would! Parishioners are often very kind to the vicarage family.

One of the kindest things someone ever did for me was when I had three babies in nappies at once. We could not afford to buy disposable nappies and I always had buckets of terry nappies soaking in the bathroom. One couple told me that they had made an arrangement with the local pharmacy: if I went there to buy disposable nappies, they would pick up the bill every month. That massive act of kindness changed my life. It happened 25 years ago, and I'd forgotten about it until I saw the couple on a social media site recently. I was able to message them and thank them for what they had done for me, even though I'd thanked them before. I do not know if I will ever be able to do anything in return, but if I saw them in need or found myself in a situation where mentioning them would be to their advantage, I'd like to think I would do so.

Most of us would think it inappropriate to remind someone of our past kindness to them and request payback, but Joseph had no hesitation in asking the person he had helped to remember to return the favour when he was in a position to do so.

We who call ourselves Christians should make it a life habit to repay the kindnesses shown to us, seeking to be kind and sensitive to others in their times of need.

Lord God, help me not to be so wrapped up in my own concerns that I forget to return the kindnesses others have shown to me in my times of need.

ALISON TEALE

All in God's good time

[Pharaoh] restored the chief cupbearer to his position… The chief cupbearer, however, did not remember Joseph; he forgot him. (NIV)

Three days after Joseph interpreted the dreams of the cupbearer and the baker, the baker was executed and the cupbearer was restored to his position. You might think the cupbearer would be excited and tell everyone what had happened in prison, but, as far as we know, he said nothing to anybody about how the prisoner, Joseph, had accurately predicted his future. Perhaps, in the fuss and busyness surrounding the feast, the right moment did not arise. Maybe Pharaoh was in an unpredictable mood and the cupbearer did not want to risk upsetting him and ending up like the baker.

There are many reasons why we fail to return favours or do good to others. The main one is probably that we get so caught up in our own lives that we forget, and the other is that the right moment does not present itself. As time goes by, the opportunities lessen and memory fades.

Two years passed in Joseph's case, but I don't believe they were wasted years. Joseph was gaining valuable administrative experience and the cupbearer was regaining Pharaoh's trust. At an opportune time, the cupbearer was prompted to remember Joseph, who was brought before Pharaoh to interpret his dream.

The outcome was that Joseph was put in charge of Pharaoh's palace. Those two years of training were thus put to good use. Joseph could not have gone easily from administering Potiphar's house to Pharaoh's palace. Experience was needed in between.

I have realised with age that we don't get where we want to go all at once. There are places where we have to stop and stay so that we can learn necessary lessons. I would like to think that Joseph did not allow himself to grow bitter for being forgotten, but accepted the time in between as a chance for personal growth.

Lord, when I am stuck in what seem like the side-roads of life, give me a heart that is willing to learn the lessons you have prepared for me there.

ALISON TEALE

The rough and the smooth

[Joseph said] 'God has shown Pharaoh what he is about to do. Seven years of great abundance are coming throughout the land of Egypt, but seven years of famine will follow them. Then all the abundance in Egypt will be forgotten, and the famine will ravage the land.' (NIV)

When you read how Joseph interpreted Pharaoh's dream, you have to admire the fact that he did not stop at giving the interpretation. He gave advice to Pharaoh about what he should do in response, so that Egypt would be prepared against disaster: 'Let Pharaoh look for a discerning and wise man and put him in charge of the land of Egypt. Let Pharaoh appoint commissioners over the land to take a fifth of the harvest of Egypt during the seven years of abundance' (vv. 33–34).

I hadn't noticed that part of the story until I read it again recently. I was rather shocked and thought Joseph was being a bit audacious. Did he utter that advice with no self-interest? Or did he see it as his opportunity to avoid being thrown back into the dungeon, planting a seed of an idea in Pharaoh's mind that might get him the role of one of the commissioners? Perhaps he even dared to hope he might be put in charge?

The interesting thing is that Pharaoh showed great wisdom himself in appointing someone with vision and understanding, because those are the people who have the inspiration to get a job off the ground and see it through. And I'm sure that while Pharaoh was waiting for Joseph to be brought up from the dungeon, he'd asked to be briefed about the man's history and what he could do.

God may have a big story that undergirds history, but he is also concerned with our individual stories. He wants us to be part of his purposes and plans. But if we don't step up, be courageous and take advantage of the opportunities that he puts in our way, we might risk being left in a metaphorical dungeon of unfulfilled promise.

'Have I not commanded you? Be strong and courageous. Do not be afraid; do not be discouraged, for the Lord your God will be with you wherever you go' (Joshua 1:9).

ALISON TEALE

The trappings of society

Pharaoh took his signet ring from his finger and put it on Joseph's finger. He dressed him in robes of fine linen and put a gold chain around his neck… Thus he put him in charge of the whole land of Egypt. (NIV)

Joseph must have felt quite strange when Pharaoh gave him linen robes to wear, put a golden chain around his neck and gave him his own signet ring. These would have been very different from the prison clothing that Joseph had been wearing for the past few years. In his early years of imprisonment, his only chain might have been a restraining ring round his neck, and manacles round his wrists and ankles would have been his only adornments (although presumably he was released from them to do his prison job).

What Pharaoh did for Joseph was to give him a uniform that would enable him to do the job he had been given without being questioned by those under his command. The clothes and accessories were a sign of his promotion and change of status. The robe would not have been of many colours, like the one his father had given him; it would have been plain in comparison, but costly rather than roughly woven wool. The chain indicated clearly to everyone his appointed office, and the signet ring gave him the right to sign off the use of various resources.

Clothing can have a symbolic meaning, and this was the case when Pharaoh gave Joseph the linen robe as a symbol of his new authority. In the same way, the prophets in the Old Testament used to wear a mantle, a large, loose-fitting garment of animal skin, to symbolise their God-given authority, and they would hand on this mantle to their successor. Today we might use the term 'mantle of authority' to denote a special anointing of the Holy Spirit for a particular ministry. We can be assured that God will clothe us with the strength we need in order to fulfil whatever task or role he has called us to.

Thank you, Lord, that you clothe us with your power from on high so that we have the spiritual resources to do your will.

ALISON TEALE

Moved to tears

He turned away from them and began to weep, but then came back and spoke to them again. (NIV)

Today's reading describes the moment when Joseph came face to face with his brothers after years of separation. Although they were older and bore the care of years on their faces, he recognised them, but they did not recognise him. Looking at them kneeling before him, Joseph remembered the dreams that had caused his brothers to plot to kill him.

We will never know what went through his mind at that moment. The desire for revenge? A tremor of anger? A twinge of hatred? Maybe a wave of sorrow? I expect he treated them the way he did to try to find out if they were sorry for what they had done. Not only did he observe their reactions to his questioning, but he spoke to them through an interpreter so that they would not know he could understand them and would thus speak freely with each other.

After he had imprisoned them for three days and they were brought back before him, Joseph was moved to tears by the concern the brothers showed for their father and their youngest brother, Benjamin. Family is family, and, whatever they had done to him, Joseph was moved with compassion by their dilemma, perhaps realising for the first time that Reuben had stood up for him all those years ago. Overcome with emotion, he had to turn away to hide his tears.

I recently visited a relative who I felt had consistently mistreated me many years ago. When I was confronted with a shrunken old lady who had no power of speech, slipping in and out of consciousness, I too forgot my injured pride, the perceived injustices and my buried anger and was moved to tears. Holding her hand and kissing her head, the unimportant things slipped away and all that was left was forgiving love.

Lord, we are human and we hurt when mistreated. Help us move beyond our wounds to the place of compassion where we can forgive and embrace those who have injured us.

ALISON TEALE

A total change of heart

[Judah said] 'Now then, please let your servant remain here as my lord's slave in place of the boy, and let the boy return with his brothers.' (NIV)

Today's chapter describes the final test that Joseph put his brothers through, in order to see if they were any different from the young men who had sold him into slavery. When the brothers were stopped on their journey home and accused of stealing Joseph's silver cup, they denied their guilt to the point of saying they were willing to become slaves and that the guilty one would die if the cup was found in his possession. It was found in Benjamin's sack.

When the brothers were brought before Joseph, Judah declared that God had found out their sin. He was not referring to the silver or the cup, but to the crime they had committed 20 years earlier in selling Joseph and misleading their father into believing the boy was dead.

Joseph saw that the brothers were changed men, because Judah was willing to give his own life so that Benjamin could return to his father, sparing the agony of the old man himself. Judah was the one who suggested selling Joseph (Genesis 37:26–27), yet now he is willing to sacrifice himself for his father and his brothers.

It was understandable for Joseph to doubt, initially, that his brothers were any different from before. The passage of years can harden hearts as well as soften them, and he needed to know which path they had taken. The weight of what they had done had obviously burdened them over the years and been a catalyst for change. Rather than hardening their hearts, they had allowed the Lord to soften their hearts to the point of total repentance and surrender.

Is there anyone you have treated badly in the past? Are you still claiming you were in the right, or are you letting God soften your heart and bring you to repentance?

'Create in me a pure heart, O God… Restore to me the joy of your salvation and grant me a willing spirit, to sustain me' (Psalm 51:10, 12).

ALISON TEALE

Pick your moment

Joseph could no longer control himself before all his attendants, and he cried out, 'Have everyone leave my presence!' So there was no one with Joseph when he made himself known to his brothers. And he wept so loudly that the Egyptians heard him, and Pharaoh's household heard about it. (NIV)

There is only so long anyone can keep up outward appearances when their inner turmoil reaches a certain level and carries on for an extended period of time. I wonder what Joseph was feeling for all those months while his brothers were away in Canaan with their father, even though they had left one of their number in prison in Egypt. Joseph must have found it hard to keep up the level of pretence and not visit Simeon, and to wait for the moment when the others returned. Not only did he have to keep up a pretence before his brothers, but also with his staff, so that word would not reach Pharaoh and perhaps compromise the situation.

Once Joseph was sure of the brothers' change of heart and could contain himself no more, he dismissed his attendants and revealed his identity to his brothers. That was not straightforward, either: they were terrified of what he might do to them. He had to repeat himself and reassure them.

During his long wait, Joseph must have thought things through deeply, because he could now see that God had used his misfortunes to position him to help his family. This fuelled his desire for reconciliation.

I have to be honest, I am an open person and I find it very difficult to keep my inner turmoil to myself, but while I was preparing to relocate to another part of the country I learnt a few lessons about the value of keeping my intentions to myself and waiting for the opportune moment to speak my heart. Unfortunately my over-eagerness in certain situations resulted in some necessary lessons, but other situations showed me that I was learning from my mistakes. And although I felt bereft at times, like Joseph, I gradually saw God was in control.

Lord, give us the strength of character and wisdom to bear the weight of keeping our own counsel until the moment is right to share our heart with others.

ALISON TEALE

Looking out for your family

So Joseph settled his father and his brothers in Egypt and gave them property in the best part of the land… Joseph also provided his father and his brothers and all his father's household with food, according to the number of their children. (NIV)

As we know, Joseph arranged for Jacob and his entire household to relocate to Egypt to avoid the famine, and, at Pharaoh's instruction, Joseph was able to give them good land on which to settle and tend their flocks. Even the family's shepherding profession worked to their advantage. When Pharaoh found out that the family tended flocks, he asked that the best-qualified of them should look after his livestock for him (v. 6).

As I write these notes, I am waiting for property contracts to be signed so that I can move from the expensive south of my country to the more affordable north. Like Jacob, I have uprooted my entire family to avoid 'the famine in the land' that threatens to drain my resources. Although I am not being uprooted due to war or famine, there are times when I feel that it is a forced migration, because there is no other choice. Two of my adult children are coming with me and two will stay behind. Part of the leaving process has involved ensuring that the two who are staying are settled in the best places for them and are prepared, practically and emotionally, for the rest of us to leave.

I stand in awe of God's provision, knowing that those of us who are moving all have occupations awaiting us. However, resettling is an ongoing process that needs persistence and commitment. Looking after your family, even when they are old enough to look after themselves, whether they be your parents, siblings or children, is a privilege and a substantial responsibility, but I am so grateful to our ever-faithful God that I have been able to help where help was needed, as well as offer moral support. Care for family is our primary Christian ministry.

Lord, thank you that you promised never to leave us or forsake us. Help us to be strong and courageous to meet the changing needs of our families.

ALISON TEALE

Put the future in God's hands

Then Joseph said to his brothers, 'I am about to die. But God will surely come to your aid and take you up out of this land to the land he promised on oath to Abraham, Isaac and Jacob.' (NIV)

Jacob died. Joseph kept his promise and took his father's body to Mamre to bury it. Once the funeral was over, Joseph's brothers wondered if, now their father was gone, Joseph would seek revenge. Jacob had anticipated this and left a message for Joseph to forgive his brothers. Joseph wept. Perhaps he was sad that, even after all he had done for his family, they still doubted that he had put the past behind him. In fact, it was his brothers who could not forget the past and forgive themselves, and their father was reaching out from beyond the grave to prevent any possible trouble.

Family troubles resurface every now and then, even when we think they are past and buried, and we often have to reassure those around us that everything is fine. As we age, too, it is natural to wonder how our children will manage without us.

I catch myself thinking that once I have downsized and relocated, my estate will be easier for my children to settle when I've gone, and that there will be something to help all of them in the next stage of their lives. Joseph, in his turn, came to the end of his life; although he was one of the youngest of the brothers, it sounds as if they all survived him. He, too, thought ahead about how his family would manage without him. However, rather than putting practical plans in place, he reminded them of eternal truths and gave them a solid hope to hold on to—that God would surely come to their aid.

Perhaps Joseph knew through his dreams what would become of the Israelites after Pharaoh's death, but this time he chose to keep his dreams to himself and leave the future in God's hands.

Lord, we entrust the lives of those we love into your hands and ask that you would help them and be with them in both good times and challenging times.
ALISON TEALE

The fruit of the Spirit

Rosemary Green writes:

When I started to plan these notes on the fruit of the Spirit, I went first to the obvious place—Galatians 5:22–23, which is Paul's list of 'love, joy, peace, forbearance, kindness, goodness, faithfulness, gentleness and self-control'. Then I asked myself, 'Is this a definitive list of the Jesus-like character qualities that he wants to develop in us over the years?' I asked my Bible study group, and several extra suggestions emerged: humility, thankfulness, thoughtfulness, contentment, wisdom, boldness and perseverance. Surely they are also qualities that the Spirit would like to grow in us. It is as if Paul dipped into a bowl of 'Spirit character' and brought out an almost random handful.

I sometimes think that we start out like hard blocks of granite; then the Creator, the master sculptor, patiently carves each of us into an individual, beautiful, living, mobile figure, as the Spirit lives and works in us. Paul prayed in Ephesians 1:19–20 (part of one of those Pauline sentences that seems to continue for ever) that we might know 'his incomparably great power for us who believe. That power is the same as the mighty strength he exerted when he raised Christ from the dead and seated him… in the heavenly realms'. Wow! The power that raised Jesus from the dead is available for me. I do not have to struggle in my own strength to change; I need to cooperate with the Spirit who works in me to bring that change, to work out what God is working in me (Philippians 2:12–13).

I see the Holy Spirit's work in our lives in three main strands:

- He makes God real to us—in our relationship with him, in worship, in Bible reading and in prayer.
- He makes God real in us as he transforms our characters—the growing fruit.
- He makes God real to others through us as we speak about him and use the gifts he gives us.

Over the next two weeks we will think about the development of 'fruit' in us—fruit that can only grow as the weeds of sin in our lives are cleared away. This will be followed by a fortnight of thoughts about the gifts he gives through the Spirit.

Prepare the ground

The sinful nature desires what is contrary to the Spirit, and the Spirit what is contrary to the sinful nature. They are in conflict with each other, so that you do not do what you want. But if you are led by the Spirit, you are not under law. (NIV 1984)

I am no gardener, but I watch my husband at work outside, and I observe the vegetable patch from the comfort of the conservatory. Even I know that before flowers or vegetables are planted, the ground needs to be dug and cleared of weeds.

I know only too well how the weeds in my own sinful nature flourish when left unattended. Before Paul writes of the fruit of the Spirit, he warns us of some of the blatant extremes of behaviour from the 'sinful nature'. At first glance, verses 19–21 look like a jungle of weeds—more reminiscent of the gutter press than of my own life. But read the list of sins slowly and prayerfully. Does any word or phrase catch your attention? Remember Jesus' warnings in Matthew 5 about the small seeds in thought or character that lie behind the visible sins.

The phrase 'fits of rage' hits me. Recently I exploded against my husband in unwarranted anger. Was it his fault that his well-meant intervention made me fail to turn off the oven, so that I burnt the contents and wasted the food? I blamed him, not my own forgetfulness. My reaction must have taken him back three decades, before the huge clearance of deep-rooted, chronic anger in my life. I thought my angry weeds had been eradicated, but a pernicious root suddenly sprouted and caught me off-guard.

'I warn you,' says Paul, 'that those who live like this will not inherit the kingdom of God' (v. 21). Does that fit of rage shut me out of God's kingdom? No, the warning of eternal exclusion from God's kingdom is for those who 'desire what is contrary to the Spirit'. But it reminds me that I must always be watchful to kill the weeds so that the fruit may grow.

Lord, I really do want to be led by your Spirit. I really do want the fruit of your nature to grow in me. Please help me to work with you to dig up the weeds of sin in my life.

ROSEMARY GREEN

Use the weedkiller

Put to death, therefore, whatever belongs to your earthly nature: sexual immorality, impurity, lust, evil desires, greed, which is idolatry… Now you must also rid yourselves of all such things as these: anger, rage, malice, slander and filthy language from your lips. (NIV)

A lot of attitudes have changed since my faith in Jesus came alive when I was a student, over 60 years ago. In our particular Christian circle, the ten commandments were doubled: thou shalt not smoke, drink alcohol, dance, go to the cinema, go to the theatre, watch TV, wear make-up, post a letter on Sunday or kiss before you are engaged. 'No sex before marriage' wasn't even mentioned; it was assumed. Younger Christians nowadays often laugh when I mention these prohibitions.

Yes, our definition of 'worldliness' was narrow; we often judged actions than attitudes. But we really were trying to please God and strive for his high standards, even if some of our thinking was distorted. Sadly, much of our secular 21st-century Western culture is similar to the hedonism of the first century, as our Christian standards and expectations are eroded by the pervading climate of a society that omits God.

We need to heed what Paul wrote to these first-generation Christians. Read verses 5–10 again, and add Ephesians 4:25–32. In these verses Paul touches on sexual impurity in thought and deed, covetousness, greed, anger, spoilt relationships, lying, idleness and gossip—and the list is not exhaustive. Does even one word strike your conscience?

Many young people wear a WWJD bracelet. 'What Would Jesus Do?' is a good question to ask in any situation as we try to please God. A member of our Bible study group had the shock of her 63-year-old husband's sudden death from a heart attack. Hearing Jesus' audible voice, 'Richard is safe with me', brought her the assurance of faith she had lacked, and she adopted WWJD as the motto for her life (without wearing the bracelet). As she says, however, 'WWJD can be a *very* hard road to follow'!

Write down any of the 'weeds', however small, that you are aware of in your own life. It is much easier to pull up weeds when they are small than when their roots have gone deep. Now ask yourself, What Would Jesus Do?

ROSEMARY GREEN

Water the seed

Blessed is the one… whose delight is in the law of the Lord, and who meditates on his law day and night. That person is like a tree planted by streams of water, which yields its fruit in season. (NIV)

When seeds are planted, they need to be watered (like the marrow seeds in our conservatory now); no water means no germination. The seed of God's word also needs to be 'watered' by the Holy Spirit if it is to bear fruit in our lives. Have you belonged to a Bible study group where, after a thought-provoking Bible discussion, Bibles are shut and the leader asks, 'Well, what prayer needs do we have today?' There is a clear disjunction between Bible reading and prayer. That is sad, because the truths that have been planted in our minds may shrivel and die if they are not 'watered in' by the Spirit as we pray. In Psalm 1, the image is of a person who loves God's law, mulls over it prayerfully, and is like a tree whose roots go deep and absorb water from the river, so that the tree is fruitful.

Bible reading and prayer need to be integrated. As Paul wrote to Timothy, 'all Scripture is God-breathed and is useful for teaching, rebuking, correcting and training in righteousness' (2 Timothy 3:16). The Spirit who inspired the writing of scripture is the one who will make it come alive for us and help us to live it out. That's logical! Any book has new meaning when we meet the author. I notice that of the four strands mentioned by Paul, only one is for our intellectual understanding, while three strands are for living. If we stray from the main road of God's way, the Spirit, through the word, will stop us in our tracks ('rebuke'), turn us round ('correct'), and take us forward on the right path ('train in righteousness'). The Spirit brings fruit in our lives through the scripture.

Read the whole of Psalm 1 again. Pray that the Spirit will show you one or two things that are particularly relevant for you today. Then take those thoughts and pray that you may live them out, to bear fruit in your life.

ROSEMARY GREEN

Let the sap flow

[Jesus said] 'No branch can bear fruit by itself; it must remain in the vine. Neither can you bear fruit unless you remain in me. I am the vine; you are the branches. If you remain in me and I in you, you will bear much fruit; apart from me you can do nothing.' (NIV)

Last year our garden had a young plum tree. An amazing crop of plums began to develop, but the fruit was too heavy and some of the slender branches broke. I tried to prop them up, even to splint them, but the sap no longer flowed, the leaves withered and the plums didn't ripen.

Before you read these notes any further, read John 15:1–12 again. Which verse stands out for you? What does it say to you about your relationship with Jesus?

I notice the last part of verse 5: 'Apart from me you can do nothing.' Nothing at all? Nothing fruitful for his kingdom. That is humbling. Separated from him, there is no sap, no life, and we wither. But then I put that phrase alongside Paul's words: 'I can do everything through him who gives me strength' (Philippians 4:13, NIV 1984). Without him, nothing. With him—with the power of his Spirit flowing through me—everything. That lifts my faith, enabling me to trust that he can make even me fruitful, in character and in action.

Other verses in our passage spell out more about the 'sap' and the 'fruit' that results from it. Look at verses 7–12. The sap flows as we stay close to him, listen to his words and obey him. Our obedience is tied up with the sap of love that flows from the Father and the Son. As we respond to that love, the 'fruit' is seen in the love we have for one another, in our witness ('showing yourselves to be my disciples', v. 8), and in effective intercession. Just one word of warning: do not take out of context the promise 'ask whatever you wish, and it will be done for you' (v. 7). Psalm 37:4 says, 'Take delight in the Lord, and he will give you the desires of your heart.' It is not about my own wishes alone; if my life is intertwined with his, I can discern what *he* wants.

Lord, I pray that I may live really close to you, with your Spirit of life flowing through me and your fruit evident in every aspect of my life.

ROSEMARY GREEN

Pruned through suffering

Now for a little while you may have had to suffer grief in all kinds of trials. These have come so that the proven genuineness of your faith—of greater worth than gold, which perishes even though refined by fire—may result in praise, glory and honour when Jesus Christ is revealed. (NIV)

I recently met a Christian Pakistani family; persecution drove them out of their own country eight years ago. They have official refugee status in Malaysia, but still hope to move on. They were deeply disappointed when they were refused entry to the USA because of the wife's Muslim background, but the husband expressed solid faith in God's good purposes for them. Meanwhile she is bold enough to use her trilingual Koran (in Arabic, Urdu and English) as a tool for evangelising Muslims.

Peter's letter is permeated with encouragement to his readers to endure undeserved suffering, patiently and graciously. As Jesus told his disciples, the Father prunes every fruitful branch 'so that it will be even more fruitful' (John 15:2). God allows suffering in our lives; it is often part of his pruning process, to make us more fruitful. Do we grumble when small difficulties get in our way? James urged his readers to be joyful when they faced trials (James 1:2). Why? Because he expected to see the fruit of perseverance, wisdom and trusting prayer. Even for Jesus, suffering tested and demonstrated his obedience to his Father (Hebrews 5:8).

I know that some of the biggest changes in me have come through hard times. Two especially come to mind. I had to fly home from South Africa with four children at the end of a superb holiday, leaving my husband in hospital with meningitis. God used that stressful time to bring a burst of fresh life into my drab spiritual state. Some years later, faithful friends spoke to the church leadership, concerned about my increasing bursts of anger. It was painful to be excluded from all ministry, but God uprooted my anger and gave me a new freedom of personality and deeper confidence in him. His pruning was indeed fruitful.

Read Hebrews 12:11. How much of the noticeable spiritual growth in your life has been associated with tough times? Pray for continuing fruit in your own life, and for friends who are experiencing hardships and battles.

ROSEMARY GREEN

Shades of grey

You were once darkness, but now you are light in the Lord. Live as children of light (for the fruit of the light consists in all goodness, righteousness and truth) and find out what pleases the Lord. Have nothing to do with the fruitless deeds of darkness, but rather expose them. (NIV)

When I got off the bus at 10.30 pm last night, it was dark. There were no street lights, and I was glad of my tiny torch as I crossed the road and walked up our lane; even more glad to get into the house and switch on the lights. The mains electricity lights the house and is also used to recharge the torch batteries.

Jesus, 'the light of the world', is our mains power, but he also tells us that we are to be the light of the world. We are his 'torches' to shine with our small lights, and we need to be recharged regularly by his power.

Paul couldn't be much clearer: 'Have nothing to do with the fruitless deeds of darkness', which are ugly and damaging in every way. 'Live as children of light' and show the fruit of goodness, righteousness and truth. We sometimes forget that the Spirit of Christ is the Holy Spirit; holiness is the prime fruit he wants to develop in us. Peter wrote, 'Just as he who called you is holy, so be holy in all you do; for it is written, "Be holy, because I am holy"' (1 Peter 1:15–16). We cannot possibly attain to the level of God's holiness, his utter purity, but that does not mean we are to be content with our shades of grey. Once we were promised that a particular soap powder 'washes whiter'; now, another cleaning aid offers us 'not one, not two, but three shades whiter'.

So I am praying that I become increasingly sensitive to any aspect of off-white unholiness in my life, however small. Every weed must be eradicated, and I want to work on every aspect of the fruit of the Spirit that we will continue to think about in the next week.

Turn 1 John 1:9 into a personal prayer: 'If I confess my sin, you, Lord, who are faithful and just, will forgive me my sins and purify me from all unrighteousness.' Thank you, Lord. May the fruit of holiness grow in me.

ROSEMARY GREEN

Love in practice

Love is patient, love is kind. It does not envy, it does not boast, it is not proud. It does not dishonour others, it is not self-seeking, it is not easily angered, it keeps no record of wrongs… And now these three remain: faith, hope and love. But the greatest of these is love. (NIV)

Thirty-four years ago, my faith was at a low ebb. I was spiritually hollow and I recognised that I knew little about loving. I read 1 Corinthians 13 and I prayed through gritted teeth, 'Lord, give me your love.' One hand was upturned; the other fist was clenched tight. If I had love, I would have to give; that seemed too hard, too costly. I stayed unchanged.

A year later, when my husband contracted meningitis in South Africa, I just began to respond to the love shown by many people out there. Home again, friends encircled me: 'Rosemary, please let us love you and help you.' But I reinforced my walls of independence: 'I'm all right, I can cope.' My husband's recovery was slower than expected, and finally their love melted my barriers. As that happened, my 'roof' came off. God's Spirit flooded me and his love poured in. Then I found that loving other people became easier as his love began to change me.

Try reading these verses in the first person: 'I am patient, I am kind. I do not envy, I do not boast, I am not proud. I do not dishonour others, I am not self-seeking, I am not easily angered, I keep no record of wrongs.' The words get choked in my mouth, because not all of them are true. But try again: 'Jesus is patient, Jesus is kind. He does not envy, he does not boast, he is not proud. He does not dishonour others, he is not self-seeking…' If the Spirit of Jesus is alive in me, he can make me like him; his loving fruit can grow in me. Through his love I have changed in many ways: I have learnt, among other things, the freedom of being forgiven and of forgiving, and of being given God's love for very unlovely people.

'Greater love has no one than this: to lay down one's life for one's friends' (John 15:13). What might this mean for you? Perhaps you can pray: 'Lord Jesus, I am scared to ask for love like yours, but I need it. So, tentatively, I ask.'

ROSEMARY GREEN

Joy in the Lord

Shout for joy to the Lord, all the earth. Worship the Lord with gladness; come before him with joyful songs. Know that the Lord is God. It is he who made us, and we are his; we are his people, the sheep of his pasture. (NIV)

'The fruit of the Spirit is… joy.' I look back to one Saturday afternoon over 30 years ago. I felt anything but joyful. My life was in turmoil after an important friendship had shattered; my trust in people was low. My husband was in America and the one daughter who still lived at home was away for the weekend. I didn't dare touch the phone; everyone would be too busy with their own lives. I was desolate, lying on the floor in tears.

Suddenly I saw the floorboards as a symbol of the Lord's solid support. I learnt a new dimension of worship and joy that day, knowing God in his trustworthiness. Even in my misery, I could have joy in him. 'Rejoice in the Lord always,' Paul wrote to the Philippians from prison. 'I will say it again: Rejoice!… The Lord is near' (Philippians 4:4–5). He knew joy in God's faithfulness, even without the psalmist's exuberance.

That is what distinguishes joy in the Lord from mere human happiness, though the two may run in tandem. My heart is lifted today as I look at the morning sunshine, a blue sky and activity at the bird table. Just surface happiness? Life is going well at present, but my happiness is rooted in deep joy.

Now read Psalm 100 again, aloud if possible. The psalmist is very upbeat. On what does his joy rest? It rests on God and his character. He reminds us, 'The Lord is God.' He is the Creator. We belong to him; we are his sheep whom he cares for and leads, who know his voice. We can 'enter his gates' because Jesus has broken the barrier between a holy God and sinful humans. His goodness, love and faithfulness are enduring. Those are just some of the characteristics of the God who gives us his joy.

Lord, thank you that my joy rests on you and on your love and faithfulness. Thank you that my joy in you can remain, even when life is hard and painful.

ROSEMARY GREEN

Knowing God's peace

Do not be anxious about anything, but in everything, by prayer and petition, with thanksgiving, present your requests to God. And the peace of God, which transcends all understanding, will guard your hearts and your minds in Christ Jesus. (NIV)

Do you have friends who never seem happy unless they are worrying? By contrast, I remember a schoolfriend who never appeared ruffled; now, over 80 and verging on dementia, God's peace continues to sustain her.

Today's verses follow on from yesterday's thoughts. 'Rejoice in the Lord' leads to two recipes for peace. Peace, like joy, rests on our trust in God's love and faithfulness. Paul's first recipe against anxiety is prayer—about everything. Nothing is too small to bring to God, nothing too big for him to handle (even when he doesn't answer in the way we would like).

Don't forget thanksgiving. Do you remember singing, 'Count your blessings, name them one by one'? Thanking God for his goodness puts our concerns into new perspective. I don't like that often-used phrase, 'Hand everything over to God', implying that one prayer should dissolve all our worries. It rarely works like that. I prefer to say, 'Invite the Lord into the situation', which gives space for a process of peace to replace anxiety.

Place your troubles one by one into God's strong, safe hands, and his peace really will guard your emotions and thoughts. The deep ocean is always peaceful, however violent the surface waves. That is how God's peace can be for us—solid calm in our hearts, however stormy life is.

Paul's second recipe is to switch our minds deliberately on to good, positive thoughts (v. 8). He is confident enough about his own teaching and lifestyle to recommend following his example (v. 9). That demonstrates peace in his own conscience.

What disturbs your peace? For me, there are two main things: nagging guilt that listens to the Accuser instead of God's assurance of forgiveness, and the cold atmosphere that follows a rare disagreement with my husband, which is melted by mutual apology and by prayer together.

Lord, please help me to focus on your generosity, your reliability and on everything that is good, so that your peace may rule in me and flow from me.

ROSEMARY GREEN

Patience and self-control

The Lord said to Moses, '… Speak to that rock before their eyes and it will pour out its water. You will bring water out of the rock for the community so they and their livestock can drink.'… Then Moses raised his arm and struck the rock twice with his staff. (NIV)

Patience and self-control are close cousins. Sadly, Moses didn't display either quality on this occasion. Even the mighty Moses had his weak spots. We might feel a bit sorry for him. Once before, God had told him to strike the rock to provide water for the thirsty, grumbling Israelites (Exodus 17:6). This time, the command was 'Speak to the rock', but instead he struck it again. Water gushed out; the Lord provided plentifully, but Moses was reprimanded for his lack of trust. A hard God, to deny Moses the privilege of leading the people right into Canaan? No, a holy God, who expects the highest standards of his people, especially of his leaders.

Sadly, I don't expect the same high standard of myself. I am aware that both patience and self-control are weak spots for me. I, like Moses, can be irritated with other people who grumble, or impatient at their inability to move faster, especially when they are dawdling in front of me. What a contrast with Jesus: he was often grieved by his disciples, so slow to grasp his teaching or to trust him, but he didn't lose patience with them. He demonstrates his Father's patience with us, seen particularly in his love that restrains the holy judgement we deserve. 'He is patient with you, not wanting anyone to perish, but everyone to come to repentance' (2 Peter 3:9).

This puts my own impatience into new perspective—impatience with a husband who doesn't seem to think it matters if dishes are not put in the right places in the kitchen cupboard, or with grandsons who bicker, trying to score points over one another. My self-control is not much better, when there is the lure of the game on the computer or the chocolate bar in the drawer.

Lord, I am ashamed of my impatience over trivial matters and my lack of self-control. I pray that I may trust, and cooperate with, your amazing, powerful Spirit to grow new fruit in me.

ROSEMARY GREEN

Kindness and gentleness

In Joppa there was a disciple named Tabitha (in Greek her name is Dorcas); she was always doing good and helping the poor. About that time she became sick and died… All the widows stood around [Peter], crying and showing him the robes and other clothing that Dorcas had made while she was still with them. (NIV)

I have a soft spot for Dorcas, perhaps because I do a lot of knitting, though my dressmaking days are over. On a first reading, we might think that the widows were weeping just because they feared there would be no more new clothes, but I'm sure their grief was over the loss of a friend who really cared about them. Although Dr Luke probably intended the story's main focus to be on the miracle, Dorcas' love and kindness are evident, even in the little that is said about her.

I don't suppose those widows were always easy to help. Many of them might have been elderly, some with set views, particular about how things should be done, crotchety in pain or fiercely independent. Was Dorcas ever tempted to be harsh or impatient with them? We don't know, but I would have been, especially when tired or when they seemed ungrateful. The fruit of the Spirit would not have been evident in all of them.

Perhaps Dorcas knew that Jesus had said, 'Come to me, all you who are weary and burdened, and I will give you rest. Take my yoke upon you and learn from me, for I am gentle and humble in heart, and you will find rest for your souls' (Matthew 11:28–29). When I am far from showing the Spirit's kindness and gentleness, I can come to Jesus, first to receive the balm of his gentleness and forgiveness for myself, then to learn from him so that the Spirit's character of kindness and gentleness replaces my own 'weed' of harshness. I want those characteristics to grow steadily in me, so that the 'gentle answer [that] turns away wrath' (Proverbs 15:1) becomes the norm in me, rather than a rare treat.

Lord, thank you that you are always with me and that your Spirit is resident in me. I know there is never an excuse for me to be snappy, harsh or unkind. Please forgive me and change me.

ROSEMARY GREEN

Truth and integrity

The Lord said to Satan, 'Have you considered my servant Job? There is no one on earth like him; he is blameless and upright, a man who fears God and shuns evil. And he still maintains his integrity, though you incited me against him to ruin him without any reason.' (NIV)

In 2016 we finally reached the conclusion of the inquest on the 1989 Hillsborough tragedy, when 96 football fans died in a crush at a football stadium. Who was responsible for their deaths? The police came out of it badly, not only for poor decisions on the match day but for the sustained cover-up of truth in the decades that followed. Some years ago, we were shocked by a scandal over expense claims by Members of Parliament, and the greed of many bankers, at times, threatens our economic stability. Where is the integrity we expect of those in public office? Even church leaders have been questioned about covering up sex scandals. It is all part of the same package of lies, greed and avoidance of guilt and shame.

We can complain vociferously about others, but we then have to ask ourselves what standards we expect of ourselves—and what does God expect of us? Jesus warned his followers not to complain about a speck of sawdust in others' eyes while ignoring the plank of wood in their own (Luke 6:41). When I read the newspaper scandals, I must also look in a mirror.

One of the names for the Holy Spirit is the Spirit of truth. He comes to teach us right doctrine, but even more important is the character of truth and integrity that he wants to develop in us. An 'integer' is a whole number, and 'integrity' implies wholeness, truth through and through.

God did not instigate Job's troubles but he did allow them. Each time, Satan went to the limits that the Lord set him. Job lost his wealth and his offspring, but he still worshipped God. Then, smitten with sores covering his body, he continued to trust God. The integrity he showed during his easy years persisted through his deep suffering, until he finally descended into self-pity and bitterness.

David, convicted of his sin with Bathsheba, wrote in Psalm 51:6, 'You desire truth in the inward being.' What do people see when they look at me? And what does God, with his X-ray eyes, see?

ROSEMARY GREEN

Faith and faithfulness

They called them in again and commanded them not to speak or teach at all in the name of Jesus. But Peter and John replied, 'Which is right in God's eyes: to listen to you, or to him? You be the judges! As for us, we cannot help speaking about what we have seen and heard.' (NIV)

Faith and faithfulness: I see a chicken-and-egg situation! Faith in a mighty God helps us to be faithful in action and speech, even in difficult circumstances. Then we experience more of God's faithfulness, and our faith grows further.

That was certainly true for these early disciples. The Peter who told a servant girl that he didn't know Jesus (Luke 22:56–57) has been transformed into the man we meet today. Two major events occurred: after Easter he met the risen, forgiving, recommissioning Jesus; at Pentecost he was filled with the Spirit. The Jewish leaders felt threatened as they saw the church growing rapidly. Peter was not scared as he stood before them, clear in his declaration of Jesus as the unique Saviour. Their feeble attempt to keep the disciples quiet was met by Peter's outspoken declaration: 'We cannot help speaking about what we have seen and heard.'

I love what happened next. Naturally, they reported the news to their friends. Most of us would probably have had a long committee meeting to discuss our plans. Not this group! They turned immediately to God in praise and prayer. First, they praised the Lord of heaven and earth (v. 24). Then they quoted Psalm 2:1–2. Read the whole of Psalm 2 to see how it continues from verse 3 onwards: they were wholly confident in God's victory over Jesus' (and their) enemies. So rather than just praying for strength to stand firm, they asked for boldness to preach. They also asked God to do more miracles, and they experienced an immediate answer.

Many of us are too timid to speak about Jesus. We may call it sensitivity or 'waiting for the right time', but to be truthful it is usually fear—and it makes us more like the Peter who denied Jesus than like these Christians, on fire for God.

Who do you expect to meet today or tomorrow? Will you pray, 'Enable your servants to speak your word with boldness'? It might be a word of testimony, an invitation to church, or a kind deed done overtly in Jesus' name.

ROSEMARY GREEN

Humility

Do nothing out of selfish ambition or vain conceit. Rather, in humility value others above yourselves, not looking to your own interests but each of you to the interests of the others. In your relationships with one another, have the same mindset as Christ Jesus. (NIV)

Paul continues to explain how Jesus set us the supreme example of humble self-sacrifice. Being divine, his rightful place was beside his Father in heaven, yet he descended down, down, down, to a criminal's excruciating death. ('Excruciating', a word describing extreme pain, comes from the Latin *crux*, 'a cross'.) That is the amazing standard of humility set by Jesus. It is a humility born of confidence—knowing who we are as children of God. It is a humility born of contentment with the gifts he has given us, so that we do not need to worry about whether others are better or worse than we are. It is a humility born of love, an aspect of the fruit of the Spirit that we thought about last week—the love that does not envy, does not boast and is not proud. It is a humility that does not argue but listens to another's opinion while quietly offering its own viewpoint.

I like to think that I share that humility. Then I think of the critical comments I often make behind the backs of those who do things differently (in other words, worse than 'my way'), or who dress inappropriately (to my way of thinking), or who run a meeting with too many songs or too few songs, too little prayer or too much prayer. It is all right to be different from others, with differing views or habits, but a slippery slope leads from 'we're different' to 'my way's better', and then to 'my way's right, your way's wrong'. That breeds disharmony, as there was between Euodia and Syntyche in Philippians 4:2, instead of the like-mindedness that Paul pleads for in our reading today. Humility? Rosemary, listen to Paul; beware of conceit, but in humility consider others better than yourself.

'Clothe yourselves with humility towards one another,' says 1 Peter 5:5. That needs to be a deliberate act, in partnership with the Spirit's work in me. Pray: Lord, I want the Holy Spirit to grow good fruit in me, while I cooperate with you.
ROSEMARY GREEN

The gifts of the Spirit

Henrietta Blyth writes:

It always seems amazing to me that when God started his wonderful rescue of the human race by sending Jesus, he only gave Jesus twelve people to work with—including a group of fishermen. If you were God and you were looking for people to work with your Son, what sort of person would you choose? I am pretty sure that experience of fishing wouldn't have topped my list.

How true it is that God's ways are not our ways! He said to Samuel, 'The Lord does not look at the things people look at. People look at the outward appearance, but the Lord looks at the heart' (1 Samuel 16:7). As God builds his kingdom, he looks at people's hearts to find his raw material. He looks for character, because he knows that we will not have to achieve great things on our own; he sends his Spirit to help us.

In the Old Testament there are lots of examples of the Holy Spirit falling on people to do great things: for example, look at Othniel (Judges 3:9–10) and Samson (Judges 15:14). The Lord said to Zerubbabel, when he set out to rebuild the temple, 'Not by might nor by power, but by my Spirit' (Zechariah 4:6). But in these cases, it appears that the Holy Spirit came as a one-off for a particular moment and reason.

Jesus told his disciples that they would do even greater things than he had done, because of the power of the Spirit, who would live with them and in them (John 14:15–21). On the last day of the Feast of Tabernacles, Jesus said, 'Whoever believes in me, as Scripture has said, rivers of living water will flow from within them.' As John explains, 'By this he meant the Spirit, whom those who believed in him were later to receive. Up to that time the Spirit had not been given, since Jesus had not yet been glorified' (John 7:38–39).

Today Jesus has been glorified and the Spirit is permanently available to all who are believers. He changes us from the inside out and equips us with gifts so that we can demonstrate the kingdom of God right here and now. These gifts will be the subject of our study for the next two weeks.

Wait for it!

[Jesus said] 'Do not leave Jerusalem, but wait for the gift my Father promised, which you have heard me speak about. For John baptised with water, but in a few days you will be baptised with the Holy Spirit.' (NIV)

God keeps his promises. Jesus told the disciples and his followers to wait in Jerusalem to receive the gift that God had promised them. They had no idea what this gift was. They didn't know when it would come or what it would look like. They thought it might mean victory over the Romans: 'Lord, are you at this time going to restore the kingdom to Israel?' they asked him (v. 6).

Jesus said it wasn't their job to know the times or dates that God has put in place, but they would receive power from the Holy Spirit, who would 'come on them' (v. 8). Then they would be his witnesses, starting in Jerusalem and moving 'to the ends of the earth'. Here is what they knew:

- There was a gift from God coming to them.
- It would be a 'baptising with the Holy Spirit'—different from John's baptism with water.
- They would receive power when it happened. This would be the power of the Holy Spirit, power from God, so it was likely to be awesome.
- As a result, they would witness to Jesus in Jerusalem and all over the world. (This may have been a frightening thought to them, given that Jesus had just been crucified.)
- Jesus would no longer be physically with them: they had seen him 'taken up'.

How did Jesus' followers feel at this point? They must have been excited, scared and doubtful (see Matthew 28:17). How did they react? They stuck together and they prayed constantly. They got themselves ready by replacing Judas on the team. They were obedient to what Jesus had told them to do: they stayed in Jerusalem and waited.

Are you waiting for something that God has promised you? What can you learn from the way the disciples waited?

HENRIETTA BLYTH

A new thing

All of them were filled with the Holy Spirit and began to speak in other tongues as the Spirit enabled them. (NIV)

The day of Pentecost was the 50th day after the sabbath of the Passover week. It was a time of celebration and remembrance of what the Lord had done in providing for his people and rescuing them from Egypt. Many Jews would have come to Jerusalem to celebrate the festival. All Jesus' followers were together in one place, probably the temple, which is why so many other people saw what happened.

The Bible tells us to watch for the 'new thing' that God is doing (Isaiah 43:19). When the Lord appeared to Elijah, 'the Lord was not in the wind' (1 Kings 19:11), but he certainly was in it at Pentecost! Then the disciples saw tongues of fire resting on each other. Such a phenomenon is not recorded anywhere else in the Bible. The disciples would probably have recognised it as a sign of God's presence, since they knew that the Israelites experienced the Lord as a pillar of fire as they travelled through the desert (Exodus 13:21).

Then the Spirit enabled them to speak in other languages. Again, this is a first! It must have caused quite a rumpus because people heard the noise and came to see what was going on. My guess is that, with the excitement and the power of the Spirit, they weren't so much speaking as shouting, and doing it in at least 15 different tongues.

The Lord had planned it so that there would be lots of foreigners present who could confirm the authenticity of the languages being spoken. This was not gobbledy-gook; people recognised their mother tongues.

We need to be prepared for God to do new things. Just because they are not what we expect or what he has done before, it doesn't mean that God is not doing them.

Has God been doing something in your life, which you have discounted because it is unfamiliar? Ask him to show you definitively whether he is acting or not.

HENRIETTA BLYTH

How do you know it is God?

[Peter said] 'These people are not drunk, as you suppose. It's only nine in the morning! No, this is what was spoken by the prophet Joel.' (NIV)

People may scoff when they see the Holy Spirit moving, and this shouldn't surprise us. In 1 Corinthians 2:14, Paul writes, 'The person without the Spirit does not accept the things that come from the Spirit of God but considers them foolishness, and cannot understand them because they are discerned only through the Spirit.' To be honest, even for those who are spiritually discerning, sometimes it is difficult to know what's going on.

1 John 4:1 tells us to 'test the spirits'. There are several ways to test whether or not something is the result of God's Holy Spirit. In these notes, I am going to explore three ways: the first is by using the Bible, the second is through the gift of discernment, and the third is by asking the spirit who Jesus is.

When the Holy Spirit came, Peter explained to the crowd what was happening by referring to the words of the prophet Joel in scripture. Making reference to the word of God is a key way in which we can test events. We need to ask ourselves: did God say this would happen? Is it in line with what the Bible says? Keep checking whether or not something is in line with what he has said. His word is always our bottom line.

Having said that, bear in mind that God is frequently doing new things, as we saw in yesterday's reading. If something happens that is not mentioned in the Bible, look at its effects; look for the fruit. Jesus said, 'By their fruit you will recognise them' (Matthew 7:16). Is the fruit good or bad?

Are you uncertain whether something that's happened is from God or not? Prayerfully reflect and apply these tests before drawing your conclusions.

HENRIETTA BLYTH

The gift of discernment

Finally Paul became so annoyed that he turned round and said to the spirit, 'In the name of Jesus Christ I command you to come out of her!' (NIV)

In 1991, I took my parents and sister to a conference in London run by John Wimber, who founded the Vineyard movement. Several things happened:

- A call went out for people with heart problems, and a friend of mine who had had a heart murmur from birth was healed: medical tests the following day found nothing wrong with his heart at all.
- The speakers talked of the world order shifting from democracy versus Communism to Christianity versus Islam. I remember thinking that was very strange, but of course now I recognise that the speakers were exercising the gift of prophecy.
- Quite a few people were receiving deliverance from demons, and occasionally there were shrieks around the auditorium. One woman behind us started shouting. John Wimber pointed at her and said, 'That is not a demon, that is hysteria; would someone please help her out of the auditorium.' It was the first time I had seen the gift of discernment in action.

Jesus spoke frequently of a spiritual realm coexisting alongside the natural realm. He sent out his disciples with these instructions: 'Heal those who are ill, raise the dead, cleanse those who have leprosy, drive out demons' (Matthew 10:8). The authority and power he gave to his first disciples, he has also given to us, and one of the gifts he has given by his Holy Spirit is the ability to distinguish between different spirits—to know whether something is of God or not. In Acts 16, Paul recognised that although the slave girl was calling them the 'servants of the Most High God' (v. 17), this was a sign not of her being filled with the Holy Spirit but of a demon's presence, so he commanded the demon to leave her in the name of Jesus.

Read Ephesians 1:18–23. God has given 'incomparably great power for us who believe'. What does this mean for you?

HENRIETTA BLYTH

Testing the spirit

No one who is speaking by the Spirit of God says, 'Jesus be cursed,' and no one can say, 'Jesus is Lord,' except by the Holy Spirit. (NIV)

Paul was keen to ensure that the early church understood the gifts of the Spirit and how to use them. At Pentecost they had all received the gift of speaking in a different language. By the power of the Spirit, Peter had preached a message that brought 3000 people to Christ in one day. (This took amazing courage: bear in mind that this was Jerusalem, where, less than two months earlier, Jesus had been crucified and the disciples had been hiding in fear for their lives.)

Paul lists a range of gifts in today's passage and makes the point that, while the gifts may be different and given to different people, they all come from the same Spirit. He also gives believers a way of testing whether a person is exercising a gift from the Spirit or not. He tells them to ask the person who Jesus is. If they are filled with the Spirit, they will respond that Jesus is Lord. If they are not, they will curse him instead.

Many years ago, I received the gift of speaking in tongues while visiting a friend who was working with Jackie Pullinger in Hong Kong. Some time later, we had gone away on retreat as a family and a pastor tested my gift by asking me who Jesus was: to my horror, out came a stream of abuse. I subsequently received significant deliverance and freedom from a number of issues that had been plaguing me for years.

Praise God that 'it is for freedom that Christ has set us free' (Galatians 5:1), and we have nothing to fear, because he who is in us is greater than he who is in the world (1 John 4:4).

What gifts has God given you? Do you have any doubts about whether any of them are from God? If so, ask a wise and Spirit-filled friend to pray with you and test the spirit behind the gifting.

HENRIETTA BLYTH

It takes all sorts

Just as a body, though one, has many parts, but all its parts form one body, so it is with Christ. (NIV)

I love God's variety, and I love the way he knows each of us so intimately. He has gifts for each and every one of us, and they are intended to enable us to do his work—to show the world who God is. The power and presence of God are seen in us as we exercise his gifts. Paul wrote, 'My message and my preaching were not with wise and persuasive words, but with a demonstration of the Spirit's power, so that your faith might not rest on human wisdom, but on God's power' (1 Corinthians 2:4–5).

It's instructive to reflect on the gifts of the Spirit displayed by the different people in Acts. As we have seen, Paul had the gift of discerning between spirits and the gift of healing. Peter, a humble fisherman, was given an amazing gift of preaching. At Pentecost, all the believers present seem to have received the gift of tongues. Ananias, who came and prayed for Paul in Damascus after his meeting with Jesus, was given an amazing gift of knowledge (and a very great deal of courage). And those are just a few examples.

The point is that we all have gifts and that the whole community of God is more than its individual parts. Together we form the body of Christ and are able to do his work: we cannot manage it alone. Apostles, prophets, teachers, workers of miracles, those with gifts of healing, those able to help others, those with gifts of administration and those who speak in different kinds of tongues—we need each other.

What are the gifts that God has given you?

HENRIETTA BLYTH

Equal opportunities

'I will pour out my Spirit on all people… Even on my servants, both men and women, I will pour out my Spirit in those days.' (NIV)

In Acts 1:14 it is clear that the male disciples joined together with all the other believers, both men and women, and at Pentecost they were 'all together in one place' (Acts 2:1). The violent wind that came filled 'the whole house': nobody missed it. Tongues of flame came to rest 'on each of them', and all of them were 'filled with the Holy Spirit and began to speak in other tongues as the Spirit enabled them' (Acts 2:2–4).

At Pentecost the Holy Spirit fell on everyone present. Gender was no barrier; age was no barrier; nationality was no barrier; previous religious belief was no barrier. Three thousand people were baptised that day, and we know from Luke's account that they came from at least 15 different countries. The amazing truth is that God made every single one of us and he loves us all equally. In Genesis 1:31 we read, 'God saw all that he had made, and it was very good.'

I have read the descriptions of Pentecost and the gifts and fruit of the Spirit many times, and I can see no evidence that God intended some gifts for a particular type of person only. He gives particular gifts to each one of us, but I cannot see that any of the gifts of the Spirit are gender- or age-specific. Indeed, the prophet Joel, writing centuries before Christ, prophesied that the Lord would be absolutely inclusive, pouring out his Spirit on young and old, men and women: '*Everyone* who calls on the name of the Lord will be saved' (Joel 2:32).

God longs to distribute gifts to everyone. Is somebody trying to stop you exercising your God-given gift? Be encouraged that 'God's gifts and his call are irrevocable' (Romans 11:29). What God has given you, nobody can take away.

HENRIETTA BLYTH

Ask for the gifts you want

[Jesus said] 'Ask and it will be given to you.' (NIV)

In 1 Corinthians 12:31 (the last verse of the passage we read on Friday), Paul wrote, 'Eagerly desire the greater gifts.' He was actively encouraging the Corinthians to want more. He also encouraged them to ask for gifts that would build up the body of Christ: 'Since you are eager for gifts of the Spirit, try to excel in those that build up the church' (1 Corinthians 14:12).

I am fortunate to have very loving parents, and I have many memories of asking for particular gifts for birthdays and Christmas. My sister, too, especially remembers asking for a giant teddy bear several times. She received a very firm 'No', and of course I didn't always get what I wanted—but I was never afraid to ask.

It is that childlike trust in God's love that Jesus is talking about when he tells us to ask. God is our loving heavenly Father and he wants to give us good gifts, particularly the gifts of his Spirit. Luke 11:13 records Jesus saying, 'If you then, though you are evil, know how to give good gifts to your children, how much more will your Father in heaven give the Holy Spirit to those who ask him!'

Go ahead and ask your heavenly Father for the spiritual gifts that you want and need. Be specific, and persevere. Jesus implies an intentionality in this passage in Matthew: ask and keep asking; seek and keep seeking; knock and keep knocking.

If you don't want any of the gifts (my mother sometimes talks about the gift of tongues being very 'unBritish' and so has never wanted to receive it), why not ask the Lord to increase your desire for them?

Ask the Lord for the gifts of the Spirit you particularly desire.

HENRIETTA BLYTH

Receive the gifts God gives you

[Jesus said] 'Whatever you ask for in prayer, believe that you have received it, and it will be yours.' (NIV)

If you are given a present, what do you do? You probably accept it, thank the giver, open it up and start using it. If it is a book, you read it; if it is a dress, you wear it; if it is chocolate, you eat it.

If you have asked God for a gift, at what point do you know you have received it? In today's passage, Jesus identifies two key conditions for receiving what you ask for from God.

The first is faith. Hebrews 11:1 says, 'Faith is being sure of what we hope for and certain of what we do not see' (NIV 1984). Our faith enables God to act, and it is faith that enables us to receive the gifts of the Spirit. We need to do things that build up our faith, and we need to ask God to give us more of it.

The second is being right with God and with each other. Forgiveness is the key to right relationship. We pray as Jesus taught us: 'Forgive us our sins, for we also forgive everyone who sins against us' (Luke 11:4).

With those conditions satisfied, how do we then exercise the gifts he gives us? You don't ask for a car and leave it in the garage: you take it out for a spin. So get going. If you have asked God for a particular gift, start exercising it. As you practise, your faith will increase and you will become better at using it. My vicar always says, 'Those who are now good preachers (or worship leaders or prayer ministers) started out as poor preachers (or worship leaders or prayer ministers) and learned how to do it better.'

Are you sitting on a gift you have asked God for, because you are too afraid to try it out? Ask a godly friend along to support you, and then go for it.

HENRIETTA BLYTH

Don't compare

[Jesus said] 'If I want [John] to remain alive until I return, what is that to you? You must follow me.' (NIV)

I don't know about you, but I am so frequently tempted to compare myself to other people. On any given day I am likely to be thinking, 'Hmm… I wonder if I'm as attractive as her?' or 'Wow, that speaker's pretty inspiring. I wonder if I'm as good?' All this comparison is very unhealthy. In contemporary culture we are constantly encouraged to compare ourselves with others, and the result is always that we either belittle ourselves or belittle other people. It is not life-giving behaviour and it's not God's way. It diminishes the gifts he has given us.

In John 21:21, Peter is comparing himself to John, and Jesus pulls him up on it. Only one thing is required, and that is for each of us to follow Jesus. We need to remember the 'audience of one': God's opinion is the only one that matters. So do not compare the gifts you have been given with anyone else's. God has a specific plan for you personally and he is equipping you with the gifts you need to fulfil that plan. There is no need for us to engage in a game of spiritual one-upmanship.

Rather than competing with each other, let's encourage one another and learn from each other. In the old days, when two oxen were yoked together to a plough, the farmer would deliberately pair up an inexperienced ox with a more experienced one. Being yoked together, the young one could learn from the elder. That's what Jesus meant when he talked about putting on his yoke and learning from him, in Matthew 11:29.

God put us together in community for a reason. We all have an opportunity to learn from others and to help others who are less experienced than we are. Who can you support and encourage today?

HENRIETTA BLYTH

Apostles and witnesses

'They triumphed over [the accuser] by the blood of the Lamb and by the word of their testimony.' (NIV)

Recently I was in the USA and visited the Billy Graham Library. I was very inspired by it. Far from being a pantheon of praise to Billy Graham, it gave glory to Jesus Christ and the word of God throughout. It made me reflect on the amazing gift of evangelism that Billy had been given. On my way out, I bought Elisabeth Elliot's book, *Through Gates of Splendour*, which tells the story of her husband and four other missionaries who were murdered in 1956 in Ecuador by the Auca tribe to whom they were trying to bring the good news of Jesus. Jim Elliot and the others were indeed among those who, as we see in today's passage, 'did not love their lives so much as to shrink from death' (v. 11).

We have seen in 1 Corinthians 12:28 that God has appointed apostles, prophets and teachers in the church. It is tempting, when we hear of people like Billy Graham and Jim Elliot, to think that God gave them an amazing gift of evangelism and that those of us who don't have it are 'let off the hook' of sharing our faith.

But even if we do not have a gift of evangelism, we can all be witnesses to what God has done for us personally. As Peter said at Pentecost, 'God has raised this Jesus to life, and we are all witnesses of it' (Acts 2:32). We can all speak of what we have seen and what we have experienced in our own lives. I believe this is what the writer of Revelation is talking about when he says, 'They triumphed over him... by the word of their testimony.'

Even if we don't have a great gift of evangelism, we can gossip the gospel. Pray for the Lord to give you one person today who you can chat to about what God has done in your life.

HENRIETTA BLYTH

Love

If I speak in the tongues of men or of angels, but do not have love, I am only a resounding gong or a clanging cymbal. (NIV)

A friend once described 1 Corinthians 12, 13 and 14 to me as a jam sandwich. Chapters 12 and 14 are all about the gifts of the Spirit (the bread) and the chapter in between is all about love (the jam). Having gifts of the Spirit is one thing, but the way you use them is another. Love trumps everything else.

Years ago, I gave a prophetic word to a friend who was having a tough time, and she was startled and upset by what I said. Praying about it afterwards, the Lord gave me a picture of rubbing salt into a wound. Salt can be used for cleansing and healing, but only if you dilute it significantly in water. If you rub salt straight into a wound, it is extremely painful. We need the living water of the Spirit to soak our gifts with love.

Love is a fruit of the Spirit. Our task is to keep asking the Lord to fill us with his Spirit, and his infilling will then pour out of us as love. We need to do everything in his strength, not our own. We need to follow him, not stride off ahead. Paul says that all our gifts mean nothing if we exercise them without love. They are worthless without love. In eternity, all the spiritual gifts will disappear: prophecies will cease, tongues will be stilled, and knowledge will pass away. When God's plans are fully realised and we are made perfect by him, we will not need any of these gifts. But faith, hope and love will remain—and the greatest of these is love.

Ask the Lord to fill you afresh with his Spirit today and for the fruit of love to be seen more and more in your life.

HENRIETTA BLYTH

God's spiritual down-payment

When you believed, you were marked in him with a seal, the promised Holy Spirit, who is a deposit guaranteeing our inheritance. (NIV)

When we believe in Jesus and receive the forgiveness that is now available to us through his death on the cross, our relationship with God is restored. This means that we will no longer have to pay the wages of sin—death—because Jesus has done so on our behalf. We can now lay claim to an amazing inheritance: we are the beloved children of God; we are all heirs with Jesus, men and women alike, and we can look forward to eternal life in perfect union with him (Romans 8:17).

The Lord has given us a sign of this, so that we can be absolutely sure that our inheritance is secure. This sign is the Holy Spirit. The manifestation of the Holy Spirit in our lives assures us that we are 'saved' and in a right relationship with God through Jesus. The Holy Spirit is like the Lord giving us a down-payment on what is to come.

As we have seen over the last weeks, the Spirit changes us from the inside out, and we see the fruit of the Spirit grow in our lives. The Spirit also equips us to do the work of God's kingdom by giving us spiritual gifts.

In Romans 12:6, Paul uses the Greek word *charismata* for the gifts. *Charis* in Greek means 'grace'. Paul is saying that a gift, a *charisma*, is an expression of *charis*, of grace. Grace is the unmerited favour of God (think of it as God's Riches At Christ's Expense).

So when we ask for the gifts of the Spirit, receive them and exercise them, we are living out God's amazing grace, and we are pointing to the eternal inheritance that is to come.

'For the wages of sin is death, but the gift of God is eternal life in Christ Jesus our Lord' (Romans 6:23).

HENRIETTA BLYTH

Use and grow your gifts

If your gift is prophesying, then prophesy in accordance with your faith; if it is serving, then serve; if it is teaching, then teach; if it is to encourage, then give encouragement; if it is giving, then give generously; if it is to lead, do it diligently. (NIV)

We need to use and develop our spiritual gifts. They are often given to us in embryonic form and we need to practise them intentionally to make them grow. In Hong Kong, Jackie Pullinger used to encourage her team to practise speaking in tongues for ten minutes every day. I walk part of the way to work; while I walk, I pray, and frequently pray in tongues. Occasionally friends have passed me and said afterwards that they could see I was praying because it looked as if I was talking to myself.

Whatever gifts you have been given, I encourage you to seize whatever opportunities you can to practise them. Sometimes it may seem a bit random, but what is the worst that can happen? I have prayed for non-believing friends in cafés, for a tree surgeon with back pain who came to work in our garden, and for friends at work. Occasionally I offer to pray for people on the train. They don't always accept, but I believe God can use the moment anyway.

Use the gifts you have been given with joy and gratitude. Here and now, as we exercise our gifts, God's presence is made known. People begin to flourish as we exercise our gifts; people begin to 'taste and see' the kingdom of God. As we are obedient and use the gifts we have been given, people get a glimpse of the spiritual realm and the truth of an all-knowing, all-loving heavenly Father. 'The kingdom of God is not a matter of talk but of power' (1 Corinthians 4:20). As we use our gifts, we demonstrate God's power.

'Fan into flame the gift of God, which is in you through the laying on of my hands' (2 Timothy 1:6).

HENRIETTA BLYTH

Friendship

Helen Williams writes:

I think my friends have found it amusing, if not a little ironic, that I've been asked to write these notes on friendship. I like to think of myself as having a lot of friends and being a good friend, too, but they will tell you otherwise. I am not good at staying in contact; I am often too busy to be of much help; I continually promise more than I can deliver and nearly always end up sending gushing texts or emails of apology. Added to that, I'm not even on Facebook. I wonder if I am fit to lead you on this journey!

What I do know, though, is that good friendships, at whatever level, are a vital part not only of our lives and well-being but also of what God intended for the building of his kingdom on earth. Against the backdrop of a popular culture that seems preoccupied with romance rather than friendship, I'm eager to see what God has to say in his word about the priority and qualities of true friendship.

What does it mean to be a friend? How do we make friends? How can we be better friends? Do we treasure our friendships? How do we, in a society heavily dependent upon social media interaction, make and develop genuinely good friendships and become true, committed friends? What about friends within our church communities? How honest should we be with our friends, and what do we do when friends let us down?

Can the Bible help us with answers to any of these questions, as we set aside the next two weeks to focus on the precious gift we call friendship? I believe there will be some challenges along the way, but much encouragement too.

In his book *Spiritual Friendship*, written between 1140 and 1167, a monk called Aelred of Rievaulx writes, 'God is Friendship.' He goes on to ask how a friendship can begin in Christ, continue in Christ and be perfected in Christ. These are great questions for us to look at, too, so let's start with God himself.

God is friendship

May the grace of the Lord Jesus Christ, and the love of God, and the fellowship of the Holy Spirit be with you all. (NIV)

In my hallway I have a print of a 15th-century painting depicting the story of the three angels who were entertained by Abraham at Mamre (Genesis 18). The three are shown eating together in close communion, and the painting (known as Rublev's icon) has long been seen as an inspiring representation of the Trinity—God the Father, Jesus the Son and the Holy Spirit: the Trinity. As in Paul's blessing for the Christian community at Corinth, we see grace, love and fellowship between the three.

Thinking about this astonishing relationship at the heart of who God is, I love one Bible scholar's description of the 'shyness' of each member of the Trinity in the icon, each pointing selflessly to the others in a gracious circle. Think of Jesus' baptism and God's voice telling his hearers to listen to Jesus. Think of Jesus telling his friends to watch out for, and listen to, the Holy Spirit whom the Father would send in his name. Remember, too, Jesus struggling in Gethsemane before his death, and yet accepting his Father's will. Could this 'shyness', this deference, this holy desire to put the other person first, delighting in them and trusting them, have something to teach us in our friendships?

In William Paul Young's novel *The Shack*, he portrays the sheer delight that the members of the Trinity find in each other's company—the celebration of life and fun, the mutual love expressed between the three. It's inspirational. I would love to be like that with my friends.

As we begin this fortnight of friendship, I believe we can do no better than to start with God the Trinity as our model: grace, love and fellowship.

Jesus asked the Father for his friends to 'be one as we are one' (John 17:11). Holy Spirit, please may that become reality. (If you have internet access, you might like to find 'Rublev's icon' and ponder what it says about the Trinity.)

HELEN WILLIAMS

God's friendship in my home

'You are my friends if you do what I command. I no longer call you servants, because a servant does not know his master's business. Instead, I have called you friends, for everything that I learned from my Father I have made known to you.' (NIV)

I wonder if any of you, like me, remember the 'Friends of God' leaflets we filled in at Sunday school. I loved them. It's an astonishing concept though, to think that we can be *friends* with the living God. Here is Jesus, in his last moments with his disciples before his arrest, and what he chooses to press home to them is that he sees them as friends.

In the letter of James, we see Abraham described as God's friend (James 2:23) and, perhaps even more powerfully, we read in Exodus that 'the Lord would speak to Moses face to face, as one speaks to a friend'. If you have time, do read Exodus 33:7–23 and 34:29–35 to understand this relationship: it's one of mutual love and honesty. Moses tells God of his fear and bargains with him, but God listens, even changes his mind and is gentle as well as empowering. It's a real relationship and a prelude to great things. Moses returns from his encounters with God, radiant with his glory.

I find this quite a challenge: when I set aside time with God, am I honest with him, willing to listen and prepared to engage? On returning to other activities, am I changed, to be like him and radiant with his glory? Sadly, I've never had to put a cloth over my head to hide the radiance, but I love the idea that, as we spend time just being with him, we begin to shine.

I love this exclamation by another Old Testament hero, Job. I wonder if it speaks to you as it does to me: 'Oh, how I miss those golden years when God's friendship graced my home, when the Mighty One was still by my side' (Job 29:4, *THE MESSAGE*).

Lord, I would love your friendship to grace my home. Teach me how to be your friend, to be brave enough to be known as your friend and to shine with your presence.

HELEN WILLIAMS

God the bond between us

Jonathan was deeply impressed with David—an immediate bond was forged between them. He became totally committed to David. From that point on he would be David's number-one advocate and friend. (*THE MESSAGE*)

In yesterday's reading we eavesdropped on the last supper that Jesus shared with his friends, where, in his words and by his actions, he raised friendship to the highest level, showing that it is at the heart of God and of his intention for his kingdom on earth. Today we look back to one of the most touching scenes in the Old Testament, in which we see Jonathan, the king's son, expressing the depth of his friendship and commitment to David, the shepherd boy, by taking off his robe and giving him his tunic, sword, bow and belt (18:3–4). Did he know, we wonder, that his new friend would one day rule the kingdom that he should have inherited himself? Like Jesus, the heavenly king's Son who washes his friends' feet, Jonathan becomes nothing so that his friend might become everything. 'Let there be nothing between us,' his actions suggest; 'we shall be undefended, open and honest.'

If we ourselves are really honest, we might admit that it is sometimes easier to sympathise with a friend's troubles than to rejoice at her successes. As we watch the story of Jonathan and David unfold in 1 Samuel 18—23, we observe in Jonathan's gift of friendship a total commitment to David's well-being and protection, despite David's growing power and Jonathan's own vulnerability. He values the friendship more than his entitlement to the throne of Israel.

I particularly love the friends' final recorded encounter before Jonathan dies: 'And Saul's son Jonathan went to David at Horesh and helped him to find strength in God' (1 Samuel 23:16, NIV). Will you pray to be the kind of person who always wants the best for her friends, no matter what the sacrifice; who prays for and senses God's purposes for them, and helps them to 'find strength in God'?

Lord, give me grace to be selfless in friendship, to pray for my friends and to help them find strength in you.

HELEN WILLIAMS

Walk beside me

Ruth replied, 'Don't urge me to leave you or to turn back from you. Where you go I will go, and where you stay I will stay. Your people will be my people and your God my God.' (NIV)

'Don't walk behind me; I may not lead,' wrote Albert Camus. 'Don't walk in front of me; I may not follow. Just walk beside me and be my friend.' Here in Ruth's story, we see a remarkable woman ready to do just that—to walk beside her mother-in-law in faithful support and love, regardless of what the journey ahead may cost her. Ruth shows a lifelong commitment to an older woman of her father's generation, going way beyond the constraints of family roles, to something that is marked not by duty but by joy.

Ruth is driven not by anything she owes to her mother-in-law (Naomi has already released her from that debt) but purely by her love for Naomi as a fellow woman and human being. The relationship is also remarkable for the way it crosses a racial divide: Naomi was a Hebrew of the chosen race, but Ruth was a foreigner, a detested Moabite. This friendship crosses both racial and religious divides and speaks powerfully of God's priorities of love and unity. These qualities are especially significant in the book of Ruth, which will end with the ancestry of King David—a genealogy that, of course, prepares the way for Jesus. Reading on, you will see the way Boaz also goes above and beyond what is expected of a family member.

When so many family relationships in our society are debased or broken or marked by selfishness, there is a challenge here to invest in our family relationships, not for anything we might get out of them but because our relatives are given to us and our lives belong together.

I know I am prepared to give much for friends, sacrificing time, money and imagination for them, while often I take family members for granted.

As you bring your family members before God now and pray for him to bless them, why not ask him if there is one who might be further blessed by your walking alongside them in friendship at this time?

HELEN WILLIAMS

What! You too?

Mary hurried to the hill country of Judea, to the town where Zechariah lived. She entered the house and greeted Elizabeth. At the sound of Mary's greeting, Elizabeth's child leaped within her, and Elizabeth was filled with the Holy Spirit. (NLT)

In his book *The Four Loves*, C.S. Lewis describes the moment when friendship is born, when two people meet for the first time and one says, 'What! You too? I thought I was the only one.' We can imagine the scene inside the humble house in the Judean hills when Elizabeth greets the young, travel-worn Mary with a 'What! You too?' kind of greeting. What joy must have followed in sharing their miraculous yet disturbing experiences of recent months! Even the baby John leapt for joy in Elizabeth's womb. There was recognition, the sharing of mutual experience and a realisation of the imperceptibly linked journey that God had called them to.

Mary may have been fleeing the anger and recrimination of her family or she may just have been seeking the friendship of the older woman; we don't know, but we do know that there was delight in their meeting. Not only that, but Mary's presence caused Elizabeth to burst into praise of God and a prophecy about the unborn child.

I love the comment of Abraham Kuyper, a Dutch theologian: '[S]he is your friend who pushes you nearer to God.' I suspect that this is what Mary and Elizabeth did for each other during a very rich three months of sharing their lives, comparing symptoms and wondering about the journey God was taking them on. When we meet people and sense that spark of connection with them, do we share our excitement about what we know of God (appropriately and sensitively, of course)? Launching in with an enthusiastic testimony may not be right for a first meeting, but I confess I rarely start any conversation by sharing how amazing God is. I'm challenged. Are we women who push our friends nearer to God?

Mary's response to Elizabeth's greeting and prophecy was to burst into her own praise of God. Why not use her song of praise in Luke 1:46–55 as a basis for your own prayers today?

HELEN WILLIAMS

A secret master of ceremonies

There is no room in love for fear. Well-formed love banishes fear. Since fear is crippling, a fearful life—fear of death, fear of judgment—is one not yet fully formed in love. We, though, are going to love—love and be loved. First we were loved, now we love. (*The Message*)

John points here to God, the source of all love (vv. 7–8), showing that God models what genuine love is (vv. 9–10) and commands us to love each other (vv. 11–12). Our love for others can only come from him.

You would think that, for Christians, loving each other would be simple, wouldn't you? How easy it is, though, to allow ourselves to be irritated by others in our fellowship or church family! Jesus knew how powerful it would be if we were all united in him: 'By this everyone will know that you are my disciples, if you love one another' (John 13:35, NIV). It would be wonderful if society could look at the Christian church and be awed by the love we have for one another.

C.S. Lewis provides a lovely perspective: 'In Friendship… we think we have chosen our peers… But, for a Christian, there are, strictly speaking, no chances. A secret Master of the Ceremonies has been at work' (*The Four Loves*). Jesus told his disciples that they had not chosen him; he had chosen them. He says to every group of Christians, 'I have chosen you for each other.' That being so, what a duty and a privilege we have to love, accept and serve one another.

'You can make more friends in two months by becoming interested in other people than you can in two years by trying to get other people interested in you,' advised Dale Carnegie in his book *How to Win Friends and Influence People*.

Both of these quotations are a powerful reminder to us that we may need to work at friendship, even (or especially) in our church community, turning on its head our tendency to ask, 'What's in it for me?'

Divine master of ceremonies, teach me to love as you love and to see those in my church family as you see them. Lead me to the people you want me to befriend, and may I be open to your prompting.

HELEN WILLIAMS

Afraid, but coming with you

[Elisha] replied, 'As surely as the Lord lives and as you live, I will not leave you.' So the two of them walked on. (NIV)

One of the most inspiring stories of friendship is that of the friends drawn together in J.R.R. Tolkien's *The Lord of the Rings*. The hobbit Merry's devotion to his friend Frodo, expressed in the words 'We are horribly afraid—but we are coming with you', leads, in the story, to the ultimate destruction of evil.

Although we know little of the friendship between Elijah and his successor, Elisha, we see this bond developing between them, in 1 Kings 19 through to 2 Kings 2. 'I will not leave you,' Elisha repeats as the long goodbye unfolds. Desperate to be as devoted to God as is his astonishing mentor, Elisha begs Elijah to share the Spirit of God within him before he is taken away. Their partnership started with Elijah's cloak being thrown over him (1 Kings 19:19); now Elisha knows that he needs the Spirit of God to cloak him.

Is there someone you look up to as a Christian, someone you trust and can be honest with, someone further along the journey and more practised in the presence of God than you are? It can be very encouraging to share our challenges and joys with such a person and to ask for their prayer and wisdom. If you don't already meet with anyone like this, it might be good to ask God to point you to someone you might ask. Equally, it could be that God is calling you to walk alongside someone who needs your companionship and discernment on their journey. 'Carry each other's burdens, and in this way you will fulfil the law of Christ', says Paul in Galatians 6:2.

In our holy friendships, are we like Elijah and Elisha, guided by the Holy Spirit (v. 2), devoted to one another (v. 6), keen to see the power of God at work (v. 8) and to become more Spirit-filled (v. 9)?

Do you remember how, when Moses was no longer able to hold his arms up over the battle, Aaron and Hur stepped in to hold them steady (Exodus 17:12)? There is strength in partnership—in holy friendship.

HELEN WILLIAMS

Sharing laughter and tears

When Jesus saw her weeping, and the Jews who had come along with her also weeping, he was deeply moved in spirit and troubled. 'Where have you laid him?' he asked. 'Come and see, Lord,' they replied. Jesus wept. Then the Jews said, 'See how he loved him!' (NIV)

I always found maths a challenge, despite my father being a mathematician, but I've no problem with the calculations of the Roman writer Cicero: 'Friendship improves happiness and abates misery, by doubling our joys and dividing our grief.'

He wrote that half a century before Jesus was born. It was true then and it's true now. When things are exciting, it's so good to share them with a friend. When life is a struggle, just telling a friend all about it can restore perspective and prevent a spiral of worry. Let's look at Jesus as he shares both joy and grief with friends.

In John 2:1–10, John tells the story of the days following Jesus' baptism, where we find Jesus celebrating at a wedding with friends and family. His being there and just happening to turn water miraculously into vintage wine suggests that he knew the importance of celebration and fun. It wasn't always easy, though: he was plagued by Pharisees or teachers of the law questioning why he ate and drank with 'sinners' (Matthew 11:19) or why his disciples weren't always fasting and praying (Luke 5:33).

In his stories, Jesus often talks of joyful friendship: just think of the parables of the lost sheep and coin. When the woman finds her coin, for example, she 'calls her friends and neighbours together and says, "Rejoice with me"' (Luke 15:9).

Jesus knew what it was to grieve, too. In today's Bible passage, we are moved by his grief over the death of his friend Lazarus (vv. 33–36) and the way he shared it with Mary and Martha, with such empathy for them as individuals (vv. 20–33). We so often read in the Gospels that Jesus 'had compassion' on those he met, engaging with them at their point of need.

In Romans 12:15, Paul tells us, 'Laugh with your happy friends when they're happy; share tears when they're down' (THE MESSAGE). Pray that your friendships may be characterised by true sensitivity and empathy.

HELEN WILLIAMS

Caring, not curing

When Job's three friends, Eliphaz the Temanite, Bildad the Shuhite and Zophar the Naamathite, heard about all the troubles that had come upon him, they set out from their homes and met together by agreement to go and sympathise with him and comfort him. (NIV)

I have a friend, a young mother, who two years ago suddenly became very ill and ended up in hospital for 16 months, much of which was spent lying on her back, totally paralysed. There has been considerable improvement since then, but she is still unable to walk and is confined to a wheelchair. I asked her what qualities of friendship she has most valued over this time. 'Consistency, loyalty and compassion,' she said, and 'people not deserting you, even when it costs them something to remain your friend'. She cites 'inconsistency, unreliability and being vague in offering support' as the most unhelpful qualities.

You remember Job? When his three friends heard of the disasters befalling him, they set out to show their sympathy for him. When they arrived, they wept loudly, shredded their clothes, put mourning dust on their heads and then sat silently with him for seven days. You can't fault such friendship, can you?

Sometimes the most powerful thing we can do is to sit quietly with a friend who's struggling. Where Job's friends went wrong was that, after the seven days, they started to try to rationalise everything, apportion blame and give advice. Much of what they said was inaccurate and most of it was downright unhelpful to Job.

Elihu, who comes into the story later, does better, holding back respectfully, then reminding the friends of God's greatness and bringing a godly clarity to the situation. Entering into the pain a friend is going through, whether physical or mental, may mean just visiting and being with them, showing you care by your presence. Asking God when to speak, and asking him for the right (non-judgemental) words to help your friend to tune into his bigger picture, could be the best gift you could offer.

Lord, you know..................., who is struggling at the moment. Show me how to be a really good friend to them. Teach me to listen closely and patiently both to them and to you, bringing your words of comfort and encouragement.

HELEN WILLIAMS

A friend with a stranger's face

One of those days Jesus went out to a mountainside to pray, and spent the night praying to God. When morning came, he called his disciples to him and chose twelve of them, whom he also designated apostles. (NIV)

'A friend may be waiting behind a stranger's face,' said the American poet Maya Angelou.

Over the years, I have been surprised by the strangers who have become friends, people with whom I've had little obviously in common, and yet with whom I have found a depth of trust, commitment and fun. In these notes, we've looked at the way God places us with friends, but I'm intrigued to see how Jesus selected his trusty friends from among strangers.

In his last prayer, Jesus says, 'I am not praying for the world, but for those you have given me' (John 17:9). How were these friends 'given' to him? If we look back to the early chapters of the Gospels, we see Jesus embarking on his ministry and meeting the people who were to become his disciples, in places as diverse as the seashore and the tax office. People started to follow Jesus around and he would regularly need to escape to a 'solitary place'. It is after one of these solitary times, Luke tells us, when Jesus had spent the entire night praying on a mountainside, that he chooses twelve special friends from among his large following. There is a clarity that comes through prayer—instructions that come after spending time just being with God.

Jesus chose his friends from many different walks and experiences of life, apparently caring more about the qualities of their heart than their rank, position or human wisdom. He didn't try to change their personalities either (think of Thomas), but worked with their uniqueness. Even to the end, he was loyal to those friends: as Judas walked forward to betray him, Jesus said, 'Do what you came for, friend' (Matthew 26:50).

Perhaps you might ask God that, when you meet someone for the first time, he will show you what part (if any) he wants you to play in the life of that person.

HELEN WILLIAMS

The best mirror is an old friend

Better is open rebuke than hidden love. Wounds from a friend can be trusted, but an enemy multiplies kisses... Perfume and incense bring joy to the heart, and the pleasantness of a friend springs from their heartfelt advice. (NIV)

On my first day at secondary school (many years ago), I met five girls who are still among my closest friends. We meet up regularly and laugh about old times, but these are friends who know me so well that they are unafraid to tell me the truth about myself. They've earned the right to do so—we've been through so much together—and I value their honesty, as well as their unconditional love. 'The best mirror is an old friend,' said the poet-priest, George Herbert.

The proverbs we're reading today describe the true friend who always loves and sticks by you 'like family' (18:24, *The Message*). We can pray that God will help us to be that kind of friend, but these verses also encourage us to offer 'heartfelt advice' and 'open rebuke' within the context of those friendships.

My schoolfriends and I have grown to trust one another, so honesty is natural, but it is something that has developed over many years. There are times when we're troubled by a friend's decision, or something they've done that is out of character, or even something hurtful they've said. Knowing whether to challenge them can be difficult. I think we must always start with Peter's words: 'Above all, love each other deeply, because love covers over a multitude of sins' (1 Peter 4:8). First we pray for love and hold our friend before God, then we ask him what to do, and we wait. Waiting gives the Holy Spirit the chance to challenge, and he is so much better at it than we are. He is, after all, the Counsellor, Comforter, Helper and Advocate. It may well be that we go on to 'speak the truth in love' (Ephesians 4:15), but let us first exercise love, patience and listening prayer.

Thank you, Lord, for the friendships that have stood the test of time. Teach me to pray for my friends and to wait for your Holy Spirit's guiding before ever launching in with advice or criticism.

HELEN WILLIAMS

Wanting the very best

My dear, dear friends! I love you so much. I do want the very best for you. You make me feel such joy, fill me with such pride. Don't waver. Stay on track, steady in God. (*THE MESSAGE*)

Words of love for his Philippian friends burst from Paul's pen, don't they? Today parts of the Christian church celebrate the lives of the apostles Peter and Paul. Sadly, it's beyond our scope here to look at all their friends—such as Luke, Silas, Philemon and Barnabas (whose name means 'son of encouragement')—but my overwhelming impression, looking through their letters and the book of Acts, is that these two men really valued the friendships they made on their travels. They show consistent concern for their friends' well-being, longing for their faith to grow and for their communities to develop in love. It's clear from many passages that their friends were devoted to them too.

I am also struck by Paul's ability to build networks between people: 'Give our regards to every follower of Jesus you meet. Our friends here say hello. All the Christians here, especially the believers who work in the palace of Caesar, want to be remembered to you,' he says to the Philippians (vv. 21–22). Helping people connect with each other, showing them that they are part of a bigger whole and have a vital part to play in a much larger story—God's story—is something I feel challenged to do.

If you have time, look at the story of Peter and Cornelius in Acts 10. There is such energy in this account of Peter, led by the Spirit, taking his friends to the centurion's house and finding Cornelius with all *his* close friends, waiting to hear the good news about Jesus. Needless to say (spoiler alert!), the Holy Spirit gets to work and Cornelius and his friends and family become the first Gentile Christians. Heeding the Holy Spirit's nudge, being obedient to God's call, bringing friends to hear about Jesus—the challenges (and encouragement) are all here.

Paul's prayer for his friends at the end of Philippians 4 is: 'Receive and experience the amazing grace of the Master, Jesus Christ, deep, deep within yourselves.' Why not take time to do just that now?

HELEN WILLIAMS

'Bear with, bear with'

It's *you*! We grew up together! *You!* My best friend! Those long hours of leisure as we walked arm in arm, God a third party to our conversation... I call to God; God will help me. At dusk, dawn, and noon I sigh deep sighs—he hears, he rescues. (*The Message*)

If you've ever seen an episode of *Miranda* on television, you will know the catchphrase 'Bear with', and it will probably make you smile. It reminds me of Paul's instruction to 'be completely humble and gentle; be patient, bearing with one another in love' (Ephesians 4:2). What else can we do when friends let us down?

The Old Testament is full of people being let down by their friends. David knew all about betrayal: psalm after psalm reveals his disappointment and anguish. Friends have always let each other down; it is part of being human. But in this age of social media and global communication, we can have so many 'friends' that it may be impossible to treasure all our friendships as well as we might. Misunderstanding and disappointment are sometimes going to happen.

If you are facing a time when a friend has let you down in some way, you could use David's words in Psalm 55 to express your 'deep sighs'. What does he go on to do? He calls to God throughout the day. What does God do in answer? He hears and rescues him. 'He will sustain you,' promises David in verse 22 (NIV).

Jesus knew exactly what it was like to be abandoned by friends. In his heartbreaking question in Gethsemane, 'Couldn't you men keep watch with me for one hour?' (Matthew 26:40) he shows just how much he understands that feeling. What does he do in his loneliness? He turns back to prayer: 'My Father... may your will be done' (v. 42).

So, we cry to God (regularly); we wait for him to hear, to answer and to sustain us. Then we go to Proverbs 17:9: 'Love prospers when a fault is forgiven, but dwelling on it separates close friends' (NLT).

Lord, I really do want to be like you, to be humble, gentle and patient and to 'bear with' friends when they let me down. Please help me.

HELEN WILLIAMS

'I had a friend'

'Love the Lord your God with all your heart and with all your soul and with all your mind and with all your strength.' The second is this: 'Love your neighbour as yourself.' (NIV)

Someone once asked Charles Kingsley (author of *The Water Babies*), 'What is the secret of your life? Tell me, that I may make mine beautiful too.' He replied, 'I had a friend.'

Over the last fortnight, we have looked at some of what the Bible says about friendship, but let's return to Jesus on the night before he died. 'I have called you friends,' he says to his disciples (John 15:15). No matter what is to come, Jesus promises loyal friendship. 'There is a friend who sticks closer than a brother,' says Proverbs 18:24, and here he is! Jesus knows he is about to lose his friendship with God (temporarily) so that we can have friendship with God. It's breathtaking, isn't it? As I accept the friendship of Jesus on the cross, I will be liberated to *be* a good friend.

There's something else that Jesus says to us about our friendships: after saying that the greatest commandment is to love God with everything you've got, he mentions the second greatest: 'Love your neighbour as yourself.' We often focus on the 'Love your neighbour...' bit as Christians, but we're not always so good on the '... as yourself'. When we accept ourselves as God sees us, understanding that we're 'fearfully and wonderfully made' (Psalm 139:14), and when we know who we are in him and where our boundaries are, we can be much better friends. It's a bit like the instruction on an aeroplane to put on your own oxygen mask before you help anyone else. It may sound selfish, but we can be so caught up in serving others that we forget to 'love' ourselves—to take time to receive God's love for us so that we can pass on that love to our friends.

Lord Jesus, thank you that you laid down your friendship with God so that I could have friendship with him. I want to be open to receive this love and to be a channel of it to my friends.

HELEN WILLIAMS

Romans

Amy Boucher Pye writes:

Many Christian figures in history named Romans as their favourite book of the Bible. For instance, the great reformer Martin Luther said of Romans that not only 'should every Christian know it word for word, by heart', but that they should occupy themselves with it 'every day, as the daily bread of the soul'. William Tyndale, a translator of the Bible, also urged his readers to learn it by heart, for 'the more it is studied, the easier it is; the more it is chewed, the pleasanter it is'. Others who were affected by reading it were Augustine of Hippo and John Wesley (see John Stott, *The Message of Romans*, pp. 19–22).

Romans has been so important over the centuries because of the deep and rich theological truths about salvation and sin that Paul shares in it. Not only that, but the latter part of his letter contains practical instructions on how to live. We can find much to stretch and encourage us as we read what the apostle wrote to the church in Rome.

He had never visited this church, but he'd heard of the divisions in it, especially between the Jewish and Gentile believers. He desired that they would find unity across their differences, and that mutual respect and love would mark their lives. After all, they were *all* sinners in need of Jesus' grace and redemption, and they were all one in Christ.

When you read, keep in mind that Paul's letter is half of the story. We don't hear the other side of the conversation—the issues that he was addressing in the church there in Rome—but we can make an educated guess. And although he wrote this letter such a long time ago to this particular context and place, yet we can find God's truth in it, speaking to us and to our situation. May we know that we are freed by the blood of Christ; that we have freedom in him, that our hope in God is a sure foundation and that we are given the gift of living as those made new.

The consequences of rebellion

The wrath of God is being revealed from heaven against all the godlessness and wickedness of people, who suppress the truth by their wickedness, since what may be known about God is plain to them, because God has made it plain to them. (NIV)

The wrath of God—not a very cheery way to open our set of readings on Romans, now is it? We often shy away from speaking of God's wrath. It feels so hard and final, especially in a relativistic society that rails against judgement and black-and-white truth. But Paul doesn't hesitate to name the major problem at the heart of the human condition: we're all sinners who need God's redeeming love and grace (as we will see in Romans 3:23: 'for all have sinned and fall short of the glory of God'). So although this passage can make for uncomfortable reading, we also can find hope in it, for it names the truth of what we know in our experience: we fail God and others and we need the Lord's grace and help.

In this passage, Paul explores what happens when people rebel against God and his laws. When they follow their own desires and refuse to bow the knee to their maker, their minds and hearts become darkened and they become fools (vv. 21–22). No longer are they infused with God's wisdom and understanding. As the Lord gives them over to their lusts, they become imprisoned by these wrongful desires and become filled with wickedness and evil: 'envy, murder, strife, deceit and malice. They are gossips, slanderers, God-haters, insolent, arrogant and boastful' (vv. 29–30).

But we can escape the consequences of our sinful actions through Jesus' sacrificial act on the cross. No longer are we defined as gossips or boasters, but as God's redeemed daughters who are filled with his Holy Spirit as they spread his love and grace. Thanks be to God!

'My hope is built on nothing less than Jesus' blood and righteousness. I dare not trust the sweetest frame, but wholly lean on Jesus' name' (Edward Mote, 1797–1874).

AMY BOUCHER PYE

The gift of the law

**Whatever the law says, it says to those who are under the law...
Therefore no one will be declared righteous in God's sight by the works
of the law; rather, through the law we become conscious of our sin.
(NIV)**

As we saw in the introduction, Paul writes to the Jewish and Gentile Christians in Rome with his radical message of God's saving plan. No matter what our racial heritage, we all fall under the curse of sin. As Paul says, God's law reveals our sinful hearts and actions, and we don't find freedom and grace through observing the law. Rather, it shows us how we fall short of God and his standards—and thus how we need a Saviour.

We so-called New Testament Christians can misunderstand God's law, thinking of it as commandments and strictures that the Lord gave in the Old Testament to keep his people in line. But God's people saw it as a source of life and joy and hope. Through it they found guidance for living life to the full. As the psalmist cried out, 'Oh, how I love your law! I meditate on it all day long' (Psalm 119:97).

I made this mistake recently when writing my BRF Lent book *The Living Cross*, and was gently corrected by the wonderful writer Michele Guinness, who combines her Jewish roots with her vibrant Christian faith. She showed me how Jesus relieves us from the curse of our sin, not from the law. After all, in Jesus' greatest commandment, he quotes from the law that God's people should love the Lord with all their heart, soul and strength (see Mark 12:29–30, quoting Deuteronomy 6:4–5).

I'm grateful to Michele for elucidating this for me, for I'm reminded that the depth of God's wisdom is so great that we will keep discovering it to be a well of living water that cleanses and fortifies us. The law brings life!

Father God, your words help us to walk in your way, and your Spirit leads us into all truth. Show me today how I can follow your life-giving law, that I might be your ambassador of love and peace.

AMY BOUCHER PYE

Saving love

This righteousness is given through faith in Jesus Christ to all who believe. There is no difference between Jew and Gentile, for all have sinned and fall short of the glory of God, and all are justified freely by his grace through the redemption that came by Christ Jesus. (NIV)

In the 16th century, Martin Luther read the book of Romans again and again in his quest to understand God's grace and the role of our works in redemption. In the margin of his Bible he wrote that this passage was 'the chief point, and the very central place of the Epistle, and of the whole Bible'. We might disagree that this section is the *most* important part of the Bible, but I think we can agree that from it we can learn very much.

We encounter here the central themes of God's plan of salvation (do read the full chapter if you have time)—that God sees us as righteous through Jesus Christ, that we all have sinned and done wrong, and that Jesus atones for this wrongdoing through his blood shed on the cross. To use more technical language, we are justified by faith in Jesus. That simply means we have been set free from the consequences of our sin—in the kingdom of God on earth and in heaven.

The gospel is a wonderful leveller, for, as Paul says, we all fall short of God's glory. We all need Jesus to save us. We cannot think ourselves superior to our family or neighbours, for we know that we are prone to temptation and sin, just as much as is the person we see caught in a cycle of destruction. We're led not to pride but to thanksgiving for the amazing way God sets us free—and we want to share this good news with others.

Read through the passage again, and try to put it into your own words. Maybe you'll encounter someone today who needs to hear of God's love for them.

Lord Jesus Christ, I think about your sacrifice of love and mercy on the cross and I am profoundly grateful. May your love mark my going-out and coming-in this day.

AMY BOUCHER PYE

The hope of glory

Therefore, since we have been justified through faith, we have peace with God through our Lord Jesus Christ, through whom we have gained access by faith into this grace in which we now stand. And we boast in the hope of the glory of God. (NIV)

'Therefore…' Paul uses this word in his letters to signify a change or a climax or a conclusion. Here in the letter to the Romans, he uses it to signal that he's moving from his discussion of how people find redemption through Jesus to the benefits of living as those who are transformed and redeemed. We who have 'peace with God' now can 'boast in the hope' of God's glory. Our salvation is assured and we are free to embrace life empowered by God's Spirit living within us. No longer do we need to be shackled to the ways of sin. And all of this is through Christ's death—he who died not only for good people but for the ungodly.

We hold on to the hope of glory, which helps us when we suffer and things go wrong. Because we live in a fallen world which is not as God intended it to be, we experience pain and the death of loved ones and disease and betrayal and so on. The Lord redeems our pain, and through our suffering we learn to persevere, our character is strengthened, and we find hope that does not disappoint.

Some Christians put such a positive spin on suffering or pain that they seem almost to welcome it. Yet how can we rejoice in cancer or heartache or any of the horrible things we experience and witness on a regular basis? I don't believe the Lord sends these things to us, but when they happen in this fallen world he's right there with us, holding us and helping us.

Today, know the assurance of the Lord that he will never leave you and that through Jesus' sacrifice you are his redeemed daughter.

'Even though I walk through the darkest valley, I will fear no evil, for you are with me; your rod and your staff, they comfort me' (Psalm 23:4).

AMY BOUCHER PYE

Our new self

For we know that our old self was crucified with him so that the body ruled by sin might be done away with, that we should no longer be slaves to sin—because anyone who has died has been set free from sin. (NIV)

The apostle Paul speaks often in his letters about the old self and the new self, as we see here in Romans. It's not surprising, for his conversion was so radical: one day he was persecuting the new church to the point of death, and the next he was blinded while travelling to Damascus, as he encountered the risen Jesus. He turned from a murderous antagonist to the gospel to one of its biggest proponents.

Paul tells the Roman church that no longer do they need to be slaves to their old life of sin; now, empowered by the Holy Spirit, they can live out of the new self. No longer do they have to be at the mercy of sin and wickedness, for they live united with the resurrected Jesus.

We might read this and lose heart, thinking that we never will win the battle with the besetting sin we face, whatever it may be. But God transforms our character day by day as we seek to live for him, and often we may not even be aware of the subtle changes that are happening within us. For example, I remember years ago, in my weekly small group, each of us describing the ways we had noticed God working in and through the other members of the group. I was surprised and heartened to hear some of the lovely things people said about each other.

We can be encouraged to know that no longer are we tied to the things of sin, but that Jesus dwelling within us makes all things new. We who have been baptised into Christ Jesus live a new life.

'You were taught… to put off your old self… to be made new in the attitude of your minds; and to put on the new self, created to be like God in true righteousness' (Ephesians 4:22–24, abridged).

AMY BOUCHER PYE

Saving hope

For in this hope we were saved. But hope that is seen is no hope at all. Who hopes for what they already have? But if we hope for what we do not yet have, we wait for it patiently. (NIV)

In my 20s, I experienced a crash in my faith when I suffered several big disappointments, including a failed romance and the falling through of a new job in a new city. In the midst of the aftermath of my shattered hopes and dreams, a friend prayed for me. She knew that I was low on hope and mentioned in her prayers Proverbs 13:12: 'Hope deferred makes the heart sick, but a longing fulfilled is a tree of life.' The simple fact of being able to name my 'heart-sickness' from my deferred hope actually *gave* me hope, for I realised that the longings I harboured might one day come true. And they did—many years later.

Paul continues to tell the church at Rome about the picture of the new life in Christ, one in which Christians are defined by hope. Though we suffer and though we fail, we long and hope for God's coming in our lives, now and in the age to come. And we see in verse 26 how God, through his Spirit, yearns with us. When we pray, we are joined by the Spirit, who intercedes for God's people according to God's will. What a winning combination that is!

During my crash of faith, I found that my stores of hope were sorely depleted but never completely empty. I knew that the Lord had the power to change me and to alter my circumstances, even if I didn't know how or when that would happen. Having a friend pray with me lifted me out of my troubles and helped me to sense that God loved me and hadn't abandoned me. I was given the gift of being able to hope once again.

Father God, when we lose hope, please send us the scripture, song or friend we need, so that we may trust in you again—and may we also bring this hope to others.

AMY BOUCHER PYE

Christ is all

For there is no difference between Jew and Gentile—the same Lord is Lord of all and richly blesses all who call on him, for, 'Everyone who calls on the name of the Lord will be saved.' (NIV)

I wonder how Paul felt when he came against his people's unbelief in Jesus as the Messiah. He could understand their reluctance—after all, he had been united with them in disbelief—and yet, once he had known the riches of Jesus as the Saviour, he must have yearned for them to understand and believe. He writes to the predominantly Gentile church, which includes Jewish believers too, to remind them that all are one in Christ. There is no dividing wall, no division between them any longer (see Ephesians 2:14). As he says in his letter to the church at Colosse, 'Here there is no Gentile or Jew, circumcised or uncircumcised, barbarian, Scythian, slave or free, but Christ is all, and is in all' (Colossians 3:11).

Today in the body of Christ we don't have the divisions of Jew or Gentile, but we face different issues that divide us. For instance, as an American living in Britain, I am often flummoxed when I come across statements of class divisions in society or even in the church. They stand out to me as foreign, and I find them difficult and sad. By contrast, in America many people see racial disunity as the besetting sin. Whether we are influenced by class or race or another issue in the country in which we live, we can work together for unity, clinging to Paul's words that 'the same Lord is Lord of all' (v. 12).

How could Christ, working through you, help you to dismantle any dividing walls in your church or community?

'Therefore, as God's chosen people… clothe yourselves with compassion, kindness, humility, gentleness and patience… And over all these virtues put on love, which binds them all together in perfect unity' (Colossians 3:12, 14).

AMY BOUCHER PYE

Our wise God

Oh, the depth of the riches of the wisdom and knowledge of God! How unsearchable his judgements, and his paths beyond tracing out! Who has known the mind of the Lord? (NIV)

Paul, a learned and wise apostle, shows his humility in this doxology as he concludes his teaching on how Jews and Gentiles are one in Christ. He quotes from the prophet Isaiah when he poses questions about who can know the mind of God or be his counsellor (Isaiah 40:13). Of course, these questions are rhetorical. No one can know God's mind—and yet the Lord has revealed himself through Christ Jesus. Through him we see an embodiment of God's wisdom.

I love the writing of Dallas Willard, who was a philosopher, concerned deeply with spiritual formation. When giving a talk at a church or at a conference, he would ask audiences who was the smartest man in the world. People would trot out answers such as Albert Einstein or other known thinkers, and Dallas would eventually say, 'But why aren't you saying Jesus?' Dallas wanted to change people's thinking and help them to realise that Jesus was and is the smartest person ever, and that he continues to be our teacher as he dwells within us.

We can become wise through the study of God's word and world, and through the indwelling of the Holy Spirit, for the Lord has created us to think and to exercise our discernment, and he will lead us into all wisdom. Whether or not we have a university degree doesn't matter when we know that we have the best and smartest teacher ever, giving us individual tutorials.

Father, Son and Holy Spirit, thank you that you teach me how to live. Help me to exercise my mind, that I would think Christianly about the world and my place in it.

AMY BOUCHER PYE

Transformed, not conformed

Do not conform to the pattern of this world, but be transformed by the renewing of your mind. Then you will be able to test and approve what God's will is—his good, pleasing and perfect will. (NIV)

The Lord is in the business of changing us, day by day. As he lives in us, he helps us to be more patient and loving, more kind and self-controlled. I think that's rather good news, don't you?

In Romans 12 we reach another of Paul's pivotal 'therefore' words. This one is great, for it signifies a change—from an exploration of the great theological concepts to their practical implications. What does it mean, then, for us as Christians to be sinners saved by grace?

To please God, we offer our bodies as living sacrifices (v. 1), not conforming to the world but being transformed by the renewing of our minds. What does that mean? One interpretation of 'offering our bodies' has to do with the sacrifices required in the Old Testament. Now, with Jesus taking away the curse of our sins, we can present ourselves as living sacrifices in the place of the dead animals once offered up. Our humble sacrifice can be made partly by heeding Paul's exhortation in verses 3–5: don't think more highly of yourself than you ought, and remember that the body has many members who all need each other.

Our transformation begins through the renewing of our minds, for our thoughts and beliefs shape our behaviour. As God's Spirit lives within us, he ushers in changes to the way we think and approach the world. For example, whereas before we may have been defined by fear or anger, now we can feel comfort and peace. Of course, transformation is a life-long process, and we won't feel perfect peace all of the time. But moment by moment, bit by bit, the Lord works in our minds, hearts and souls. As we centre our thoughts on him, we are changed.

Lord Jesus, mould me and shape me; make me anew. Renew my mind, that I might bring you glory.

AMY BOUCHER PYE

Love in action

Be devoted to one another in love. Honour one another above yourselves. Never be lacking in zeal, but keep your spiritual fervour, serving the Lord. Be joyful in hope, patient in affliction, faithful in prayer. Share with the Lord's people who are in need. Practise hospitality. (NIV)

When my husband and I were first married, we had some dear friends round for dinner. When I popped to the kitchen to grab the green beans, my husband served Steve some sparkling water. Well, he thought he was pouring sparkling water, for that's what the bottle said, but when I walked back into the room I exclaimed, 'That's the radiator water!' Our car was old and we needed to carry water with us to top up the radiator; somehow the bottle for the car had made it to the dining-room table. Steve said with a smile, 'I see you are heeding Paul's exhortation to practise hospitality! You may need more practice!'

We all need practice at living well, don't we? (And I hasten to add that the water we eventually served was clean, although not sparkling.) Paul's instructions in just these few verses can be held close to our heart as we seek to live godly lives. He tells us to love each other, honouring our neighbours above ourselves; to serve the Lord with enthusiasm and passion; to keep our joy strong and to pray faithfully; to open our homes and share with those who are in need; to bless, rejoice, mourn, be humble, and live peacefully with everyone.

I wonder how the world would change if we could implement even a small percentage of these commands. Truly the world would then know that we are Christians, through our love in action.

Might you choose one or two of Paul's instructions to practise today? Perhaps, too, you might be inspired to memorise this passage.

Lord God, you give us the resources we need to live well, including these practical instructions. May I take them to heart today, that I might live for your glory.

AMY BOUCHER PYE

Submitting to authority

Let everyone be subject to the governing authorities, for there is no authority except that which God has established. The authorities that exist have been established by God. (NIV)

This passage has sparked much debate over the years. When Paul calls for obedience to the government authorities, does he therefore imply that we should obey a tyrant such as Hitler or Stalin? The agreed answer is 'No.' Although Paul calls for the Roman Christians to be 'subject to the governing authorities', he doesn't have in mind that they should move outside God's laws and practices in their obedience.

I find it interesting that so much ink has been spilt on the exception to this rule, rather than discussing what submission to the state means. We need just and good governments in the world to exercise authority, and perhaps in the West we take for granted all the good that we have in our governments—especially when we can so easily see the failings in other political systems. But to live in a country where the rule of law is observed, where individuals are presumed innocent until found guilty, where education and health and safe roads and so on are provided through our taxes, is a gift we often overlook.

How can you pray for your government today in its local and national expressions? What about the ruling authorities of other countries, which you know to be corrupt or bankrupt? Perhaps you could become involved in local affairs, or with a national political party. Christians will fall along the whole spectrum of political commitments, but we should be voicing our views and embodying God's truth as we try to make the world a better place.

Father God, you are the fairest judge and you rule with wisdom and grace. May those in authority over us exercise your wisdom and justice.

AMY BOUCHER PYE

The clothes of Christ

The night is nearly over; the day is almost here. So let us put aside the deeds of darkness and put on the armour of light. (NIV)

Although Paul's conversion story was dramatic, as we explored last week, we see in his writing that he also acknowledges the continuing process of sanctification that followers of Christ engage in throughout their lives. Paul uses the active forms of verbs when describing how we put on the new self and take off the old self in Ephesians 4:22–24, and he does the same here when saying that the Roman Christians should 'clothe themselves with the Lord Jesus Christ' (v. 14). Just as we get dressed daily, so should we 'put on' the clothes of Christ.

Do you ever consider what these clothes may be? In verse 12 they are described as the 'armour of light', which we can put on as our culture becomes increasingly dark and troubled. Paul gives us other images of Christ's clothes in his letter to the Colossians, where he says, 'Therefore, as God's chosen people, holy and dearly loved, clothe yourselves with compassion, kindness, humility, gentleness and patience' (Colossians 3:12).

Let's consider some of these. When we put on compassion, we're putting ourselves in someone else's shoes: the roots of the word, after all, mean 'to suffer with'. Kindness is obvious, but easy to withhold—for example, when we fear that our act of kindness might be rejected or misunderstood. Can we wear this virtue without worrying about how it will be perceived? Humility means viewing ourselves neither as nothing nor as too much. We see that we are made in God's image and are therefore priceless, but we also know that we are sinful and need his grace and mercy every day.

I invite you to wear the most beautiful clothes ever!

Lord Jesus, I want to take off the rags of bitterness and anger and put on the royal robe that you give me. I know I am your beloved child; help me to live out of that identity this day.

AMY BOUCHER PYE

The weak and the strong

You, then, why do you judge your brother or sister? Or why do you treat them with contempt? For we will all stand before God's judgment seat. (NIV)

Some friends of ours are Christians who have come to Christ out of a Hindu background. Having been vegetarians their whole lives, they continue the practice of not eating meat—but, as one of them says, 'Of course, now that we follow Christ we could eat meat if we wanted to.' I appreciate the way she states the matter: although she is no longer under the laws of Hinduism, she is now neither forced to eat meat nor forced to abstain. She has freedom in Christ.

Paul was concerned about the division in the church at Rome, mainly between the Gentile and Jewish Christians, and how the former were looking down on the latter for sticking to their lifelong practices of following the Jewish dietary laws. Paul has words of exhortation to both parties. To the Gentile Christians he says, 'Stop showing contempt', and to the Jewish Christians he says, 'Don't judge those who eat everything.' God alone is our judge and we should leave the pronouncements to him.

We might find ourselves falling into bad habits of judging in little, subtle ways. Perhaps we don't shop on Sundays but we know other Christians who do, or we hold to a doctrine that others disagree with, and we're certain that we are right and they are wrong. Whatever the matter, we can follow Paul's instruction to seek the kingdom of God, which is filled with righteousness, peace and joy in the Holy Spirit (v. 17) as we 'make every effort to do what leads to peace and to mutual edification' (v. 19).

'Let the peace of Christ rule in your hearts, since as members of one body you were called to peace. And be thankful' (Colossians 3:15).

AMY BOUCHER PYE

God's call

I will not venture to speak of anything except what Christ has accomplished through me in leading the Gentiles to obey God by what I have said and done—by the power of signs and wonders, through the power of the Spirit of God. (NIV)

As Paul wraps up his letter to the Romans, he adds the longest closing remarks to be found in any of his letters—partly, scholars think, because he had never visited this church before. He tells of upcoming travel plans and implores the church to support his missionary efforts. Note his laser-like focus on what he perceives as God's calling on his life: he is a 'minister of Christ Jesus to the Gentiles' (v. 16). He has, with God, determined what his unique mission is in life, and all that he does reflects that calling, as empowered by the Spirit.

Have you considered what your special calling is from God—what your mission is in life? When we have a sense of what it is, we can more easily say 'yes' or 'no' to requests that we receive. Of course, sometimes we need to help out at church or in the community with tasks that are outside our immediate calling and gifts, because there is a lack of resources to meet those needs (for example, I help with the children's ministry at my church). But we feel most alive when we are doing what God has called us to do—whether that's providing meals for the homeless or leading a business or running a toddler group.

If you'd like to explore this issue more, I highly recommend Os Guinness's book *The Call*. In a series of short chapters and engaging stories, he examines not only our calling but the one who calls us and loves us. 'Now to him who is able to establish us in accordance with Paul's gospel, the message he proclaims about Jesus Christ, to the only wise God be glory for ever through Jesus Christ! Amen (after Romans 16:25–27).

Giving Father, loving Son and comforting Holy Spirit, thank you for your never-ending love for me. May I live and love and learn and bring you glory, now and always.

AMY BOUCHER PYE

Dealing with worry

Bola Adamolekun writes:

When I was asked to write these reflections on dealing with worry, I could not have imagined how special they would become for me. A month before the time I had set aside to prepare them, I found myself so deeply challenged by several issues that I felt unable to choose a way forward. I felt bewildered and betrayed—it was not a fun place to be in.

On the way to work, I was reflecting on one of the Bible passages I'd chosen, devising in my head what to write about it. The same evening, I realised I needed to live by that passage if I was to get through my situation sane and emotionally intact. This set of reflections has therefore become more personal and more challenging to write. However, I am not claiming to have the issue 'sussed', and it's very likely that sometime in the future, someone will remind me of the advice I'm giving. I hope that, as the things I've learnt are helping me through this period of transition in my life, the same will be true for you, now and in the future.

I've approached the question of dealing with worry from a variety of angles. Anxiety can come at us from different places and at different times. So we start with a brief look at a character in the Bible who had to deal with a challenge. Then we move to some of the more well-known biblical passages on coping with worry, to see what they might mean for us. Finally, we look at some of the responses we can make to anxiety.

My prayer, for you and myself, is that these reflections may lead us deeper into the wholeness and peace of Christ.

Transition and the 'worrying' itch

The Lord said to Joshua… 'Moses my servant is dead. Now therefore arise, go over this Jordan, you and all this people, into the land that I am giving to them, to the people of Israel.' (ESV)

'Moses my servant is dead.' Dread words for a dread situation. Joshua was undoubtedly still grieving for his great leader, mentor and friend when he was commanded to take up the reins, to follow in Moses' steps in the leadership of Israel. Of course, he had been training for this: after all, Moses had transferred his authority to Joshua before he died. However, the reality of stepping up can often bring out hidden insecurities. I imagine that Joshua looked over at the people who had caused Moses so much grief and gulped. Perhaps his first reaction was, 'Nope, I'm not ready for this.'

What do you think about God's words to Joshua in this passage? Reading it, I get the impression that, perhaps, in addition to grieving, Joshua paled, clasped his hands over his head and wondered what he had let himself in for. Who would want to lead such a quarrelsome, querulous people? The first time I heard about Joshua, he was presented as a model of a fearless leader who trusted in God. But in God's exhortation to him, that doesn't appear to be the case—at least, not at first. God will need to tell Joshua three times to be strong and courageous (vv. 6, 7, 9).

Here is Joshua, with all the training he has received, bolstered by the trust, support and affirmation of Moses and the Israelite people—and yet he was probably worried and afraid. What if he failed? This wouldn't have been a paranoid, self-indulgent question. Moses, that great leader, hadn't managed to get into the promised land, so how could Joshua be expected to do any better?

Worry is like an itch: scratch it and it grows until our anxiety is all that we can feel.

Are anxieties crowding out your peace of mind? Write them in your journal or pin a list of them up where you can see it. It's time to bring them out of the dark and into the light.

BOLA ADAMOLEKUN

Leaning

[God said to Joshua] 'I'll be with you. I won't give up on you; I won't leave you. Strength! Courage!' (*THE MESSAGE*)

It appears from these verses that Joshua was indeed worried. Was he worrying that he might fail? The encouragement to be strong and courageous comes straight after God has told Joshua that he will be with him and will never abandon him.

If we are worrying, it shows that we don't really believe that God will get us through the difficulties we're facing. Being courageous means not being discouraged by threatening situations. We need to face up to risk and pain, because they are a part of our journey, however much we might want them not to be. I often aspire to a 'pain-avoidance' path, but that actually means I'm looking for a 'growth-avoidance' path—sad but true.

Strength, in this situation, means resisting the itch to worry, resisting the seductive belief that by thinking about it all the time, we are doing something about it. Think if you must, but also pray—and, most importantly, surrender.

Where do we find this strength? God says that he will be with us, so the strength simply has to come from him. On occasion, strength may come through our friends and families, but worrying can often isolate us, cutting us off from the support of other people. God tells us to be strong, and I believe that he is also saying we must lean into him to find that strength.

Maybe we don't have the money to pay our bills, or we can't find the solution to a particular conflict or get ourselves out of a tricky situation, but God is still with us. He is still not giving up on us; he is still alongside us. In most cases, we will only understand this later, when we look back at the situation. For today, though, remember: 'Strength! Courage!' God is with you.

Dear Lord, please help me to hope, to be patient, to trust and to remain constant as I lean into you. Amen

BOLA ADAMOLEKUN

Cold comfort

[God said to Joshua] 'From the wilderness and this Lebanon east to the Great River, the Euphrates River—all the Hittite country—and then west to the Great Sea. It's all yours. All your life, no one will be able to hold out against you. In the same way I was with Moses, I'll be with you.' (*The Message*)

I have a confession to make: it doesn't come easily to me to offer comfort. I was once sitting across from a woman on the train who was grieving as she talked about a relative she had left in hospital. As I listened and felt her pain, I found I could say nothing. Everything in my head sounded trite, and I worried that it would all be cold comfort. So I said nothing; I just listened to her on that train journey.

Imagine if Joshua, on hearing that God's promise to Moses had passed to him, had thought to himself, 'Well, that's cold comfort. Didn't Moses fail, even with God's promise?' He could have felt justified in continuing to worry or even refusing to move forward with the job he'd been given. But instead, Joshua started to act, by giving orders to his officers and his people.

Rather than believing and trusting God's words about who we are, we often believe and trust in our own circumstances and limitations. Worse still, we see the limitations of other people and accept them as our own: 'Well, if they couldn't do it, what chance have I got?' We then become paralysed by worry.

On the train that day, instead of worrying about saying the wrong thing, perhaps I should have just tried to offer comfort, praying that, if I failed, it wouldn't cause lasting damage. I should have trusted that God would bring true comfort and teach me how to do better next time. Perhaps the right words—or even just 'OK' words—would then have come out of my mouth. Instead, though, I worried. In effect, I was placing my own feelings ahead of the other woman's need for comfort.

When we worry, we lose perspective.

For more ideas about gaining perspective, read about Elisha and his servant when they were under attack, in 2 Kings 6:14–17.

BOLA ADAMOLEKUN

Jump if you dare

So humble yourselves under the mighty power of God, and at the right time he will lift you up in honour. Give all your worries and cares to God, for he cares about you. (NLT)

God cares about us. That's the clincher, isn't it? Do we truly believe that God cares—not in a benign but distant way, but actually getting involved in our lives? The Amplified Bible adds the words 'with deepest affection, and watches over you very carefully'.

In Jesus, God broke into the world when we were still so very imperfect. Surely, then, no problem is too small or too trivial to bring to his attention, or so monumental that he can't resolve it. Peter's instruction to 'humble yourselves' (v. 6) is also crucial: it means putting aside the 'me first', 'my way', 'how I think it should go' attitude, and trusting that God will act to bring me through.

On a couple of occasions, I have seen my life-plans break into tiny jagged pieces. I have been so shattered by the experience that it has been impossible even to talk to God without carrying those sharp pieces in my mouth. So I cannot offer a trite, happy-ever-after testimony, but I can tell you what today's Bible passage says to me.

It brings to mind a dance move in which one dancer flings herself with total abandon at her partner and he catches her before they segue into the next move. It requires total trust that, as she leaps, her partner will be there to catch her. In his letter, Peter is encouraging us to choose to abandon ourselves and jump, so that we are no longer dancing solo but are moving with a partner.

This is also the movement of a distressed child who flings itself into the open arms of a parent. The Lord of the Dance catches us if we dare fling ourselves at him.

Lord, here I am. Catch me, for I need you to hold me, to carry me through this situation and bring me home safe. Amen

BOLA ADAMOLEKUN

Clothing makes the woman

[Jesus] said to his disciples, '… Consider the lilies, how they grow: they neither toil nor spin, yet I tell you, even Solomon in all his glory was not arrayed like one of these.' (ESV)

I work at a university part-time and often have to bite my tongue when I see what some of our female students wear. I tell myself that it's a different generation, a different age, but I also remind myself that we are all just working this life out, trying to figure out our place in it. Sometimes the clothing we choose to wear helps and sometimes it doesn't. I know that during my own student days, clothing played a much larger role in my life than I care to acknowledge—and sometimes it still does.

Often, when we decide what we are going to wear, we are trying to control the way we are perceived and received by others. Of course, there are exceptions: sportswear is chosen for comfort and ease of movement; winter jumpers are meant to keep us warm. However, our clothes can sometimes move beyond their main function of covering us up. An interview suit, a smart casual outfit, a wedding dress—these are all examples of clothing whose function is to direct the way we want to be seen, to explain the role we want to play in our own story.

In Jesus' words about clothing, he is teaching that we should not worry about meeting our basic needs, but I think we can stretch the application to mean that we shouldn't worry about how we are received and perceived by others. I don't mean that we stop wearing appropriate clothes for the situation; I do mean that we might choose to give up trying so hard to control the way we are perceived by other people. We might all dress differently on the outside, but on the inside we should all be alike—choosing to resemble Christ.

How do you marry being made in the image of a creative God with your choices about your outer appearance?

BOLA ADAMOLEKUN

Designer life

[Jesus said] 'Wherever your treasure is, there the desires of your heart will also be.' (NLT)

I came across an internet meme (an idea or concept that spreads rapidly on social media), while trawling Facebook instead of working. It show-cased a number of famous individuals whose careers did not take off until they were middle-aged or older. Some weeks later, I came across an interview with one of these individuals, where he made a flippant remark about money. I wondered how this person's desires had changed since he became a household name.

Treasures are the things we prize and value most highly. They might be objects, ideologies or people. Some of our treasures and things that we know we care deeply about, but there are also treasures that we remain unaware of until a threatened or actual loss makes them known to us.

What if our treasures are linked to the kind of life we hope for in the future? I suspect that, for many of us, our desires are far from reality, and within that distance between dream and achievement lies the 'worrying' itch. We may not be consciously anxious, every day, about how to reach our goal, but the further that desire is from our reality, the greater our susceptibility to worrying about it.

We cannot read what Jesus says here about worrying without asking the question, 'What do I treasure, and who is watching over those treasures?' If we ourselves are watching over them, then we are likely, sooner or later, to become anxious about our treasures. We are not all-powerful, all-knowing and everywhere—but we do know someone who is. Give him your treasures, and let him do the anxious watching.

Ask God to reveal the hidden treasures of your heart and where they are located. Perhaps it's time to hand them over to him, whether for the first time or not.

BOLA ADAMOLEKUN

What is your sight fixed upon?

[Jesus said] 'Your eye is like a lamp that provides light for your body.'
(NLT)

Telling someone not to worry, when they have big questions in need
of answers, is like offering a small plaster to a large gaping wound. Life
brings big questions. What's the easiest way to have nothing to worry
about? It's simple. Do nothing, and you will have little or nothing to worry
about—except, perhaps, boredom and a gradually creeping frozen state.

So we are choosing life, right? And a small plaster won't do. If you do
have big questions that are keeping you up at night, please *talk* to someone—preferably a safe person who can help you keep the perspective of a
disciple of Christ. If our eyes are the windows to our soul, sometimes we
need a little window-cleaning. (And if you are the person being asked to
do this for someone else, please clean tenderly but firmly.)

Every now and then, I am gently prodded and reminded that I need to
surround myself with people of faith—people who help me to remember
who I am in God's eyes and where my focus should be located. If I look at
the world and let that determine my perspective on life, a tidal wave of
worries and anxieties will soon head my way. How could it not? There are
big issues in our world, so there are big questions to go with them.

The big questions of life are not unimportant to us as Christians. But
if we are worried about them, perhaps the turning point might be (as
today's verses remind us) to re-examine our perspective. Could it be time
to turn our eyes in a different direction?

---

*Have you recently examined your focus—what you see and how you build your
perspective on life? Do you see hope or dismay? Where do you need to turn?*

BOLA ADAMOLEKUN

'I can't help it!'

[Jesus said] 'So don't worry about tomorrow, for tomorrow will bring its own worries. Today's trouble is enough for today.' (NLT)

When I mentioned to some students that I was reflecting on worrying, they asked for help, because even at this stage of their lives they are already prone to substantial anxiety. They said things like, 'I can't help it'; 'I'm not really worrying, I am just thinking about it'; and 'I just want things to be perfect.' When I speak to parents, including my own, I hear something similar in the context of their children's lives: 'What will happen to him or her if I don't worry?'

Jesus tells his disciples, including us, not to worry. He says it four times in today's Bible passage. Quite clearly, we should not be scratching at the itch, and yet we still do.

Are we worrying because we want to fix things, make things better or control things? It is no coincidence that this particular part of Jesus' teaching comes after he has asked us to examine what we treasure, what we focus on and how we understand life. These are all discipleship questions.

The passage as a whole reminds us that God sees us and cares for us. Therefore he will not let us be without the things we need. He will make sure we have them if we entrust ourselves to him and to his plans.

Material things are important, but God's kingdom ought to be far more important to us. This is part of what it means to worship him and to allow him to be sovereign over us. Perhaps, if we let go of trying to get what we want and trust God to give us what we need, we might find we have more than we thought we did.

From the list of burdens, challenges and anxieties you wrote down last week, what do you think you may be trying to control? Is it time to surrender these things to God?

BOLA ADAMOLEKUN

Breathe, pray, breathe, wait, breathe...

[Jesus said] 'I have said these things to you, that in me you may have peace. In the world you will have tribulation. But take heart; I have overcome the world.' (ESV)

One of the things I have had to learn in following Jesus, and have found myself learning repeatedly, is that the presence of God's peace does not mean the absence of trials or anxieties. Being human and living in a broken world guarantees trials—even though, as I mentioned last week, I would much prefer to live a trial-free life.

A path of total ease and freedom from worries, I suspect, would lead us to become frozen: it would actually prevent us from becoming people who are made fully in the image of God. It's not that God sends us trials and anxieties to make us better people, but following Jesus means living as he did. He was born into a broken world; he entered into desert temptations; he faced opposition and the ultimate sacrifice, with tears. Jesus chose to follow the Father, and in doing so he chose to follow a calling that would inevitably bring about the opposite of ease and freedom from troubles.

I am challenged daily by the fact that being a disciple of Christ ought to change the way I respond to trials and anxieties. I try not to deny that the problems exist; instead I remind myself that God knows my many frailties and failures and that he is still there, even when other people are not.

I try to breathe through the fear and worries, and I find it helpful to do this a day a time, confessing the fear, talking to God about it, and trying to keep my mind on the fact that God has a plan.

This, for me, is what it means to be brave, to choose to focus on what is good, to choose to trust God, and to choose to be thankful. What does being brave mean to you?

Jesus has overcome the world. How would you live this out, day to day, in the presence of your challenges?

BOLA ADAMOLEKUN

The importance of lament

Open your ears, God, to my prayer; don't pretend you don't hear me knocking. Come close and whisper your answer. I really need you.
(*THE MESSAGE*)

Sometimes, all you want to do is rail at the world and its injustices, particularly when those injustices are the root of your troubles.

You are doing your very best, standing, holding up a positive face, hoping, praying and then… it gets worse. And you think, fine, I'll just keep on. But at night, awake in your bed, there's that thought, that question: 'How long, Lord? How much longer? I'm not sure I can keep keeping on.'

Sometimes it's important to lament, to cry, to break down and yell. What, though, when an injustice comes from a person who is very close and intimate, one to whom you have entrusted yourself and your vulnerabilities? What do you do? Does the worrying intensify? Do you think, 'If only…'?

Sometimes, the pain turns you on your head and you can't help but feel your anxieties closing you down. The psalmist is clear: when that happens, he calls on the Lord to hear him, to defend him, to vindicate him and clear the path ahead. He rails against the cause of his pain, even as he cries out to the Lord for safety. To be worried is to be anxious, troubled and disturbed; and when the cause of it is a difficult relationship, it takes a lot out of us. There is nothing as hurtful as a painful, bullying, manipulative or troubled relationship.

Please cry, lament and spill your heart out to God, and then… wait on him. In verse 22, the psalmist says, 'Pile your troubles on God's shoulders—he'll carry your load, he'll help you out.' So gather together the sharp edges of your pain, pour it all out before God and wait. He will help.

Lord, help me to forgive, to let go, to surrender and to find a place of safety in you. Amen

BOLA ADAMOLEKUN

The magnitude of praise

I praise God for what he has promised. I trust in God, so why should I be afraid? What can mere mortals do to me? (NLT)

Our work environment can be a place of significant meaning. It can be the place where we explore our values and identities through what we produce or contribute. How we work, collaborate and compete with people adds to our understanding of who we are. We can spend about a third of our waking lives at work, so it's no surprise that when work is not going well, it bleeds deeply into our personal lives and affects our health and emotions. Toxic workplaces can become a constant source of debilitating anxiety.

The psalmist, in today's reading, is surrounded by enemies, and yet he makes a positive choice. Will he surrender to his fears? No! Will he lament? Yes, but he will also praise God.

What does this mean? Praising God, within this narrative, is about entrusting ourselves into his care. It's about reiterating to ourselves that our vindication and protection come from him. It's about choosing a perspective that says there is a much bigger player in what's happening to us, and that player is *for* us.

These are brave words; they are also hard words where the toxicity of our environment expresses itself in workplace bullying or where the spectre of job loss hangs over our heads.

If we choose to praise, are we just in denial? No! To praise means to sing the truth of who we are and the story we are in. Praising God when everything has gone wrong is about telling God, and ourselves, that we know it is not the end. There is more going on than the eye can capture, so we praise him.

In God, whose word I praise, in God I trust and am not afraid. What can mere mortals do to me? In God I trust and am not afraid.

BOLA ADAMOLEKUN

The grace of being thankful

Sing to God with thanks in your hearts. Do everything you say or do in the name of the Lord Jesus. Always give thanks to God the Father through Christ. (NIRV)

Have you ever started a prayer of thanks, only to find, halfway through, that you had started petitioning God? Maybe this only happens to me, but when it does, I ruefully apologise and start again. It's strange to say that, living in a world with plenty, thanksgiving can often be less joyful than if we live in a world that has much less.

I grew up in the Nigerian Anglican Church and, believe me, nothing poured dismay into the heart of a child who was yearning for the church service to be over, like the announcement that a thanksgiving was about to take place. This was not a polite prayer of 'Thanks very much, Lord, because you are wonderful.' If one person was about to give thanks to the Lord, it was a call-out to all their family and friends and polite acquaintances—even strangers were welcome. Cue a procession to the altar rail, with a slow shuffle dance, to be followed by prayer, more prayer, a chorus of 'Amens', then more dancing before going back to the pews. Then we would start all over again, because it was rare for just one family in the congregation to be giving thanks.

It may be trite, but it's true, that there is something powerful in being thankful. It helps us pick up the various blessings we've forgotten or taken for granted. It helps us remember that all good things come from God. Thankfulness switches our hearts from what we lack to what we have received. It is Christian mindfulness. It relocates our perspective, realigns our standing and reminds us to worship the Lord of glory.

As today's Bible passage says, talk to God, tell him what's going on and practise the grace of being thankful. His peace will follow.

Can you commit to making a prayer of thanks every day from today? What would your thanksgiving procession look like?

BOLA ADAMOLEKUN

The knowledge gap

For, 'Who can know the Lord's thoughts? Who knows enough to teach him?' But we understand these things, for we have the mind of Christ. (NLT)

Most of my working week is spent with non-Christian colleagues, and our conversations are pretty frank. There are some conversations where I come up against a knowledge gap: explaining the Trinity is never going to be easy. However, I strive to bridge that gap, trying to explain things from my point of view—and, to be honest, I sometimes have no idea whether they get it or not.

Paul, in today's passage, says that there are two types of wisdom—the wisdom of the world and the wisdom of those who have accepted the cross of Christ. My colleagues and I share many similar views but, every now and then, we hit a crossroads and head off in separate directions. Often, when that happens, the difference between the two types of wisdom is clear.

But, what happens when it's not so clear and you haven't a clue where 'wisdom' lies? Sometimes, you have a problem and you're trying to explain to a friend exactly how it's affecting you. You're not looking for sympathy, but you think it would be nice to get some kind of sympathetic response. Instead, though, your friend explains to you why you shouldn't be worrying about the issue, and that makes you want to bop them on the head with a feather duster. The verse printed out above reminds us that there are times when words cannot explain what we are experiencing, the way it makes us feel, or how it seems to steal the breath of life from us.

The Holy Spirit knows us and knows God, and I think that wisdom is found when the gap between us and God is bridged—or simply when the deep, uncomfortable space within us is soothed by the Spirit of God. We don't have the answers as yet, but we know they will come.

Waiting on God is a part of our discipleship journey; it is also our worship.

BOLA ADAMOLEKUN

Onwards

[Jesus said] 'I am leaving you with a gift—peace of mind and heart. And the peace I give is a gift the world cannot give. So don't be troubled or afraid.' (NLT)

Once, when I was recounting the challenges ahead of me, a friend asked me, 'Do you believe that God is good? Do you believe that God is faithful— that no matter what you do, he is there rooting for you? Do you believe that God is present and that he wants the best for you and will work to bring it about?'

How would you respond? I ask this because, as I see it, we have a choice: either we believe everything my friend was saying, or we believe that the circumstances surrounding us are far greater than God's goodness, faithfulness, presence and abiding love. If I told you that the key to soothing the 'worrying' itch is to believe in God's presence, what would you say? What are you thinking about it? Better still, whose thoughts are you thinking? Whose thoughts surround you daily?

'Don't be afraid,' the Lord says. 'I've got this situation in hand and I've got hold of you. Walk with me and we can do it together.'

You've made mistakes. We all have. We make errors of judgement that stay with us daily, but, when all is said and done, we are children of the ever-loving, ever-faithful, super-abundant, forgiving, merciful, gracious, gentle yet firm, all-knowing, all-seeing Lord of heaven and earth, who says to us, 'Be strong and courageous.'

He knows how fragile and weak we can be, how life can throw up painful and challenging circumstances, and so he sends his Spirit to help us through it. Sometimes, 'coming through' means seeing dire circumstances to our right and left, but gritting our teeth and holding on to the Lord. And he holds on tight, even if you let go.

Be strong and very courageous; let his peace take hold of you.

Lord, you are good and faithful and you love me beyond anything I can imagine. Please send your Holy Spirit to be with me. From today onwards, I choose your peace over the 'peace' of this world. Amen

BOLA ADAMOLEKUN

'Bless you': the Beatitudes

Bridget Plass writes:

The Beatitudes, the first part of Jesus' Sermon on the Mount, are a favourite part of our liturgy. The words are beautiful, but there is a danger that, taken as a whole, they can become a cosy familiar list, making it easy to skate over the challenges and promises that Jesus was offering the crowds gathered on that hillside and still offers to us today.

One thing is for sure, it wasn't a Galilean supermarket deal: 'Buy this and you win a free gift.' Certainly, the free gift of salvation that Jesus offered was pure blessing with no strings attached, but there are many challenges that follow on from it: in the kingdom of heaven, every blessing comes laden with responsibility. When the angel Gabriel said to Mary, 'Greetings, you who are highly favoured', we are told immediately that she was deeply troubled (Luke 1:28–29). When we read the Beatitudes, we are seeing into the heart of Jesus' kingdom and everything his life on earth stood for. He lived here as one of us, so, whatever he is asking of us, he knows both the cost and the blessing.

So what are the Beatitudes? Maybe the nearest we can come to a definition is to say that they are the rock on which the kingdom of God is to be built. They are intended to shock us: they turn our assumed values upside down. They did then and they do now. But they also give a clear insight into everything that mattered to Jesus. In one very important sense, when we look at these blessings, we see the heart and passion of Jesus, and we can't really miss what it will mean for us to be salt and light in our often flavourless and dingy world.

Can it be true?

**'Blessed are the poor in spirit, for theirs is the kingdom of heaven.'
(NIV)**

What did he say? Blessed are the what? Can't you just imagine the ripple of excited bewilderment passing through the crowd seated on that hillside so long ago. They knew the rules. The religious leaders, the devout ones, those blessed with riches, the Roman occupiers—surely they were in charge of the kingdom. Luke, recalling the same incident, has Jesus saying, 'Blessed are you who are poor' (Luke 6:20), leaving out the words 'in spirit'—but for the crowds, who had been brought up to believe that riches could be equated with blessing, the message was the same. We— the losers, the sinners, the outsiders, the semi-educated working class of the day—are in. We—the sick, the women, the children, the slaves, those with no keys to any door, let alone the kingdom of heaven—are in.

And for us today? Sadly, the message still needs to be heard, as some big churches get bigger and wealthier and some of the little ones struggle, both financially and numerically. Many people we meet would say, 'Just getting by day by day can be very, very tough; we are holding on to our faith by a thread.' But Jesus is saying, 'You are in!'

My husband Adrian and I have recently returned from a tour in Australia, where we spoke at a variety of churches. Our favourite was the church we visited in the suburbs of Sydney. Outside was a huge placard with the words 'No Perfect People Allowed'. Different words, same message. All you who are humble enough to recognise your strengths and weaknesses, who don't think you are better than anyone else, who know you are hardly spiritual giants, who realise you need God to top up your faith—good news! The kingdom of God is for you!

Father God, so many of us feel pretty useless today. Help us.

BRIDGET PLASS

Chin up!

'Blessed are those who mourn, for they shall be comforted.' (NIV)

I don't think this is an instruction; rather, it's a statement of fact. Entering fully into the dangerous world of another person's sorrow is the inevitable consequence of loving enough. The word 'compassion' means 'shared pain', and when we care deeply for someone whose heart is breaking, ours will not stay intact. But if we mourn for and with others, does that mean we too will receive God's comfort?

The professional mourners outside the house of Jairus in Matthew 9:23 were not engaging truthfully with his pain and neither needed nor received comfort. However, to catch a profound truth about mourning, you only had to witness the outpouring of grief and joy from friends, family members and supporters on the steps of Liverpool Cathedral, on the day last year when the victims of the Hillsborough football disaster were vindicated. Kenny Dalglish's quotation from the Gospel of John, 'I will never leave you or forsake you', along with the words of the Liverpool football chant 'You'll never walk alone', acknowledged a truth that many communities have learned in tragic times: shared pain brings comfort. When we realise that other people's tragedies could have been ours, we understand what Paul meant when he said of the body of believers, 'If one part suffers, every part suffers with it' (1 Corinthians 12:26).

There is a sense of belonging in shared grief that creates community, breaks down the barriers of isolation and loneliness, and opens us up not only to comfort but to be comforted.

Just recently, someone told me of her experience shortly after her mother died. After six weeks she returned to her slimming club and shared the reason for her absence. 'Chin up!' said her instructor, who then wrote in her notes, 'Counselled client over loss of mother.' Like Jairus' mourners, the instructor neither embraced shared grief, not received comfort!

Father God, help us to be brave enough to let our hearts go out to those in pain, and help us to acknowledge the joy and comfort of belonging to a grieving community.

BRIDGET PLASS

Meek, not weak

'Blessed are the meek, for they will inherit the earth.' (NIV)

Surely this does not mean 'Blessed are the doormats who let the world wipe its boots on their beliefs' or 'Blessed are those who keep their mouths shut and don't make a fuss.' Maybe we have been lulled into believing that the words 'meek' and 'weak' are interchangeable. That's the way the world we live in can make us feel as Christians—feeble and irrelevant, with our emphasis on love and our alliances with the marginalised.

So what do we mean by 'meek'? Perhaps a clue lies in the extraordinary juxtaposition of prophetic words used in Zechariah 9:9 to predict the entrance of Jesus to Jerusalem: 'See, your king comes to you, righteous and victorious, lowly and riding on a donkey.' The donkey, as the humblest means of transport, symbolised Jesus' triumph and victory over the bullying distortion of the Jewish law and the superpower mentality of the Roman occupation.

Who are your modern-day heroes? Mine include Nelson Mandela and the young Pakistani girl, Malala Yousafzai, two of the many who choose to lay down the weapons of revenge and offer instead the undeserved but precious jewel of forgiveness.

Jesus says, just a few verses later, 'Blessed are those who are persecuted because of righteousness, for theirs is the kingdom of heaven' (Matthew 5:10). As prince of heaven, Jesus could—as he told Peter in Gethsemane—have called down twelve legions of angels, the elite troops of the ultimate superpower, to save him from arrest (Matthew 26:53). Instead he chose the way of persecution—torture, humiliation, death and seeming failure. But while the Roman empire has long been swept away, the kingdom of Christ endures for ever. And Jesus' followers, however bullied, ridiculed and disregarded they may be, can stand tall as rightful heirs and possessors of the kingdom.

Father God, help us never to lose confidence in everything you taught us, and never to give in to the temptations of a world that equates meekness with weakness.

BRIDGET PLASS

Sticky toffee pudding?

'Blessed are those who hunger and thirst for righteousness, for they will be filled.' (NIV)

What are we most hungry and thirsty for nowadays? What satisfies us? Judging from all the cookery programmes on television, it's a mixture of deconstructed puddings and tortured vegetables. Restaurants have decided we will only be satisfied if our meat is thoroughly 'pulled'.

In another sense, we might say we hunger and thirst after experience. We run marathons. We hurl ourselves from heights, attached to elastic. We jump out of planes. Popular presents include vouchers for every adrenalin-powered activity on the planet. But righteousness? That's probably not at the top of everyone's birthday wish list.

Interestingly, the Greek word *dikaiosyne* can mean both 'righteousness' and 'justice'. Righteousness is about one's own relationship with God, while justice is about caring what happens in the wider world. Ideally, of course, the two go hand in hand. The closer we get to God, the more we hear the beat of his heart for justice in his world—a world that, at the time of Jesus, was ruled by a combination of Jewish and Roman imperialist laws. Jesus challenged both, standing on the words from Isaiah 61:1–2: 'The Spirit of the Sovereign Lord is on me, because the Lord has anointed me to proclaim good news to the poor. He has sent me to bind up the broken-hearted, to proclaim freedom for the captives and release from darkness for the prisoners, to proclaim the year of the Lord's favour.'

The answer to spiritual satisfaction lies in a conversation that Jesus had with his disciples, seated by a well in Samaria. When asked if he was hungry, he replied, 'My food is to do the will of him who sent me' (John 4:34). If we genuinely hunger and thirst after the will of our Father, to stand against injustice and for righteousness, maybe sticky toffee pudding or skydiving will come a poor second.

Father God, help me to spend a little time today looking at my appetites. What do I long for? What will make me satisfied? Then show me something you want me to do for you today.

BRIDGET PLASS

What do they see?

'Blessed are the merciful, for they will be shown mercy.' (NIV)

What did the sceptical and the curious see when they looked at members of the very earliest church? We are told they were so deeply impressed by the love shown between the believers that thousands were converted. What did Paul see in Stephen's eyes as he was stoned brutally to death? Hope, certainty and forgiveness—qualities that Paul found extraordinary, which he had never experienced, despite keeping the law for the whole of his life.

So, what do the sceptical and the curious see when they look at the church today?

While we were in Australia, we spent time with a wonderful group of young charismatic Catholic Christians. They were experiencing an unusual mixture of despondency and elation as they contemplated the way the world was responding to their part of the church family. On the one hand, there was the public humiliation of television interviews with a cardinal who confessed to his involvement in a long cover-up of the sexual abuse of children by a young priest. It was sordid, sad and all too familiar. Who would want to be associated with that?

On the other hand, they were revelling in the initiatives set in place by Pope Francis. He is the 'real deal'—as he showed the world at Easter 2016, publicly washing the feet of refugees, Muslims, Jews and non-believers, giving out 100 sleeping bags to the homeless and installing showers for them in the Vatican. 2016 was the jubilee 'Year of Mercy', when the pope wanted all believers to have 'a genuine experience of God's mercy, which comes to meet each person in the face of the Father who welcomes and forgives, forgetting completely the sin committed'.

We love because he first loved us. Are we offering love and mercy in Jesus' name to a broken world? Are we defined by mercy?

Lord, help me to see how the world sees me today, so that I can begin to clear out anything that is preventing the people I meet from coming closer to you.

BRIDGET PLASS

Eye recognition

'Blessed are the pure in heart, for they will see God.' (NIV)

The other day, some friends and I got idly on to the subject of tattoos. 'What about those people who get tattoos all over their faces? Do they have to get a new passport?' one of us asked. No one knew the answer, but we did agree that, with eye recognition technology, the facial resemblance was no longer so vital.

It started me thinking about the way God sees us. Jesus said, 'Your eyes are like a window for your body. When they are good, you have all the light you need. But when your eyes are bad, everything is dark. If the light inside you is dark, you surely are in the dark' (Matthew 6:22–23, CEV). He knew who could see spiritually, and it wasn't those who thought they were getting everything right. Many of the Pharisees reckoned they could see extremely clearly, loudly criticising those they judged to be blind—but they never once cottoned on to who Jesus was or to the fact that he was doing his Father's work in the world.

As often with Jesus, there is a paradox in his words. By acknowledging that we are partially sighted because of the huge grubby planks in our eyes, we become able to see a bit more clearly (Matthew 7:3–4). And what lovely things we see when we bypass outward appearances. When our children were small, we survived many long car journeys by playing 'Guess famous people in 20 questions'. Our daughter was three. 'I've got one,' she would always chirrup, 'beginning with P.' Her brothers would kindly try to eke out the questions, knowing full well who she was thinking of. 'P' was our wonderful friend whose learning difficulties and physical problems rendered him invisible to many others. But his sweetness, gentleness and care for everyone he met made him, for my daughter, the most famous person in the world. In him, we all saw a glimpse of Jesus.

Dear Father God, please help me to open my eyes so that I bypass my prejudices and preconceived ideas and catch a glimpse of you in the people I meet today.

BRIDGET PLASS

Peace at any price?

**'Blessed are the peacemakers, for they will be called children of God.'
(NIV)**

Our first two sons have very different personalities. The eldest couldn't
stand it when a nice time was interrupted by naughty little brother, but
his younger sibling found it very difficult to give in and say sorry in order
for peace and fun to be restored. 'Can't I say sorry for him, Mum?' eldest
would plead, and got very fed up when I tried to explain why that wasn't
OK. The restoration of pretend peace wouldn't have brought closure and
hugs of forgiveness for my little miscreant. Peace at any price couldn't be
an option.

The crowd sitting on the grass thought they understood what 'peace
at any price' meant. They had it inscribed on their coinage: Augustus Caesar, 'Prince of Peace', 'Bringer of World Peace'. They knew that their faith
and their temple were tolerated as long as they didn't disrupt the uneasy
truce. No wonder the religious leaders found Jesus dangerous, to the
point of wanting him dead. Peace at any price was their preferred option.

So what does it mean to be a peacemaker? Jesus promised to leave us,
his children, peace, but he said, 'I do not give to you as the world gives'
(John 14:27). Not pretend peace, then, but *shalom*—a word that covers
peace, harmony, wholeness, completeness, prosperity, welfare and tran-
quillity. This was a peace based on forgiveness, that would be life-giving
and transformative for a troubled world.

Of course, when it came to the crunch, our Prince of Peace was prepared for 'peace at any price'. The price of peace? His death, for us, on the
cross. There could be no higher price than that.

---

*Father God, help us today to look for opportunities to bring genuine active
peace into any situations where we find ourselves.*

BRIDGET PLASS

The book of Proverbs

Ann Warren writes:

I have to confess that in the past I have spent very little time reading the book of Proverbs. I knew that friends were currently reading some part of this book every week. But while Proverbs was obviously having a deeply helpful effect on them, its significance had somehow passed me by—until I was asked to write these notes. As I read the book through in greater depth, I finally realised what a wonderfully valuable source of inspiration and wisdom I had been missing.

This amazing collection of wise sayings was written down during the time of the 'Kings', several hundred years before the birth of Christ. Around 500 of the sayings can be attributed to the wisdom of Solomon, but biblical scholars now believe that they were actually written by a number of different wise people over this period.

The proverbs are not necessarily promises or fixed rules about life; they are simply wise and timeless advice about how to make life work better for you. Above all, they are wonderfully practical and down to earth.

Poetic couplets like those in Proverbs were a normal form of communication in the Hebrew culture of the day, making a statement and then repeating it in a slightly different way or contrasting it with another to make a memorable impact. They are very practical, colourful and often humorous sayings that linger in the mind long after we have read them. The book of Proverbs never minces words and there is seldom any doubt about its meaning. 'Like a gold ring in a pig's snout is a beautiful woman who shows no discretion' immediately conjures up a vivid and unmistakable picture!

Other proverbs look below the surface of life and echo our pain and deeper longings—for example, 'Even in laughter the heart may ache, and joy may end in grief' or 'The purposes of a man's heart are deep waters, but a man of understanding draws them out.' There is a timeless wisdom in these words which will stay with us. In reading some of these proverbs together, I hope and pray that we will come to experience a new vision of what God is saying to us.

Trust in God alone

Trust in the Lord with all your heart and lean not on your own understanding; in all your ways submit to him and he will make your paths straight. (NIV)

'Get wisdom,' says the book of Proverbs—and even if it costs you everything you possess, make sure you obtain it (Proverbs 4:7). Why? Because the possession of wisdom will sustain you for the rest of your life.

After many years as a counsellor, frequently asked for my advice, I have occasionally made the mistake of imagining that I know most of the answers. But God alone knows the unspoken heartfelt needs of each person and what lies ahead for her in the future. I most certainly do not. Most of us will have encountered wonderful old people who radiate wisdom, whose advice and help we would completely trust. But this same God-given wisdom is available for all of us if we only seek it with all our hearts.

How out of tune this sounds with the contemporary search for fame and money, which is so much more central in people's lives today. While wisdom is of great value in every part of life and will carry on into eternity, fame and money are temporary and transient. Many a famous actor or wealthy sportsperson coming towards the end of their time in the spotlight must dread the downward spiral from whatever fleeting status they have achieved.

In contrast, let us take the hand of the God who loves us more than we'll ever know, and he will give us the wisdom we need to make our life paths straight. It's not about self improvement or learning a new skill, but about trusting the age-old wisdom of God: 'When the Lord takes pleasure in anyone's way, he causes their enemies to make peace with them' (Proverbs 16:7).

Lord, teach me to trust you in all my ways and to seek your wisdom. Amen

ANN WARREN

I want it now!

A person's wisdom yields patience; it is to one's glory to overlook an offence. (NIV)

The virtue of patience does not fit very easily into today's world. We are all in such a hurry to cram everything into our impossibly busy lives that it seems we seldom make time to listen properly when someone is talking to us.

'To answer before listening—that is folly and shame' (Proverbs 18:13). However justified it may seem to us at the time, impatience is usually rooted in the desire to get on with what we ourselves want to do, without interruption, so that we can meet our own urgent needs as quickly as possible. But if we allow this feeling to take over, we will have little room left for people and situations that really need our full attention.

It is hard to emphasise strongly enough how important it is to listen to our children and to others in need. This was brought home to me one day when I had been helping out in our local food bank. A very troubled woman had been pouring out all her worries to me while waiting for her supplies. Sadly, there seemed to be very little that I could do to help her, apart from listening, so I just sat there, intent on what she was saying and praying silently while she talked.

Afterwards I was amazed to hear what she had said to the manager as she left: 'That was the very first time that anyone has ever taken the trouble to really listen to my problems, and I am feeling so much better already.' It was a lesson that I would not forget. Sometimes, just caring enough to listen is all it takes.

Heavenly Father, please give me the patience to find time to listen to friends and family when they need to be heard, and always to remember how much you love them.

ANN WARREN

The value of discipline

Start children off in the way they should go, and even when they are old they will not turn from it. (NIV)

These memorable verses stand in complete contrast to the contemporary wisdom of the 21st century: 'Go with the flow' and 'If it feels right, do it.' Probably we have all been affected by the laissez-faire climate of the age, being urged to let children follow their own inclinations—such that talking about discipline can sound seriously out of date. Or perhaps we think of discipline as some kind of harsh routine or daily deprivation.

Discipline, though, is the key to making the most of our lives. Until and unless children practise and hone the skills they have been given, they will never achieve real success. Just look at the training and discipline of successful sportspeople, and how many hundreds of hours it takes to become a champion athlete or ballet dancer.

When children are allowed to follow their own natural instincts—to take what is not theirs, to hurt and bully people they do not like, or just to sit on the sofa and watch television or play with their computers all day—the consequences can be seen all too clearly around us.

One thing I have found incredibly helpful from these verses is the encouragement to trust that, however far from God our grown-up children may have strayed, if we have brought them up in the way of faith, they will return to it one day. I have personally seen this happen several times now, when 40- and 50-year-old sons and daughters of Christian friends, who had almost lost hope for their children, have suddenly returned to their early faith in the most amazing ways.

Heavenly Father, please give us the wisdom and sensitivity to train up the children entrusted to us in the way they should go, to preserve their precious faith amid all the unbelief that surrounds them in today's world.

ANN WARREN

Avoid temptation

**Can a man scoop fire into his lap without his clothes being burned?
Can a man walk on hot coals without his feet being scorched? (NIV)**

There are many passages in Proverbs warning young men about the temptations of loose women and prostitutes, but you may ask, 'What relevance does this have for us?'

I think there is probably more temptation on offer to everyone today than in any bygone age. There are endless gambling websites that can be secretly used in the privacy of our own homes, every kind of pornography to tempt curious young people, dating agencies that attract not only singles but also disillusioned married people in search of a 'change', and then of course the availability of all sorts of drugs for a quick fix on a night out. We need to be on our guard against all of these, however harmless others may make them sound.

Probably we all like to think of ourselves as proof against temptation, but if we are honest, each one of us has our own particular weak spots and our personal fears and vulnerabilities. We live in a world that is morally bankrupt, where all kinds of temptations will be continually pulling at us—and where 'the enemy' is all too well aware of our weak spots.

Few people are strong enough to make good moral choices in the heat of the moment, so here in Proverbs are some important points. First, do not 'scoop fire into your lap' or put yourself in a position where it is much more difficult to avoid being tempted. And second, make up your own mind exactly what you will do, well before any possible temptation has come your way. In other words, make decisions in advance, and stick to them, come what may.

Heavenly Father, please help us to follow your ways, and protect us from the temptations that assail us on every side.

ANN WARREN

Always speak the truth

The Lord detests lying lips, but he delights in people who are trustworthy. (NIV)

A person with a corrupt mouth is called 'a troublemaker and a villain' in Proverbs 6:12, and Proverbs 10:31 tells us that 'a perverse tongue will be silenced'.

I wonder if you have ever exaggerated a story in order to make it sound better than it really was (a journalist's stock in trade), or made some harmless-sounding promise, such as 'We'll get together soon', when you actually have no real intention of doing so? Have you ever twisted the facts to make someone's actions sound worse than they really were?

Most of us will have felt uneasy or conscience-stricken if we have ever succumbed to this kind of temptation, but if we are not careful, exaggerating facts and making empty promises can soon become a dangerous and destructive habit.

Exaggeration can lead to a trail of greater dishonesty. To me, it is frightening to see that in today's society lying is often viewed as a completely harmless and even skilful thing to do—that is, if you can get away with it.

God is a God of light and purity, and he cannot live with our half-truths. So, if we have even the slightest tendency to distort the truth, we need to come before him and repent, genuinely committing ourselves to crystal-clear honesty.

Someone has suggested the need for a lie-check facility on our mouths—perhaps a bright red line that shines out clearly when we distort the truth! More realistically, we need the Holy Spirit, the Spirit of truth, to anoint our minds and our mouths so that we will be known as people who always speak truth.

Ask God to show you ways in which you have been tempted to water down or distort the truth, and pray for wisdom as to how to deal with this temptation.

ANN WARREN

Speak the truth in love

The tongue that brings healing is a tree of life, but a deceitful tongue crushes the spirit. (NIV 1984)

As we saw yesterday, one of the clearest messages in Proverbs is that God detests 'lying lips' or dishonesty of any kind, and this verse points out how a tongue that brings healing is actually a 'tree of life'.

I can think back to times when friends have had the courage to tell me when they thought I was going wrong, and would probably have experienced great difficulty in finding the courage to speak up like this—as most of us would.

Sometimes we can convince ourselves that our wrongdoing is harmless, and at such times we really need honest, trustworthy friends to bring healing by pointing out the error of our ways and gently putting us back on the right track. We must not keep silent when we ought to speak up, however difficult or uncomfortable it may be for us. What a tragedy it is when truthful words are withheld!

This is especially true if we are speaking up in a group of people where others are attacking God and all of us who believe in him. However, it is essential on such occasions to speak kindly and not to sound antagonistic. One of the ways that works best is just to tell them, calmly and lovingly, that God is very important to me. They then realise that I am not attacking them, just taking personal responsibility for my faith.

The minute we allow ourselves to get uptight about this kind of witness, we are in dangerous waters. We will be communicating nervousness and anxiety through our body language, which is often stronger than we realise. Again, we need the indwelling grace of the Holy Spirit.

Try to think of ways that you could naturally speak in love about your faith, without communicating fear or stress.

ANN WARREN

Build strong marriages

May your fountain be blessed, and may you rejoice in the wife of your youth. (NIV)

One of today's greatest tragedies is the collapse of marriage right across society, leaving single-parent families struggling to survive and children without a much-needed father or mother.

How do so many couples get into this situation? Do they spend too little time together, or fail to make one another feel special—'to rejoice in the wife [or husband] of their youth'? Sadly, much of the secular advice on the subject of marriage focuses too heavily on sexual satisfaction and not enough on how to help one another through the up and downs of this most crucial relationship, which is the foundation stone of our society.

Even Christians sometimes assume that, since they are both believers, all will be well—but building strong marriages can be quite hard work and many people need a great deal more help than they are likely to have been given. A good marriage will never 'just happen' without our putting a lot of time and prayer into the relationship, and too many Christians who are dutifully carrying out their primary ministry outside marriage discover it far too late.

When my late first husband and I hit a difficult patch in our relationship, we had no idea where to go to find help. In addition, we felt very afraid that we might be letting God down if we even admitted to having problems—a feeling that, unfortunately, is not at all uncommon.

Thankfully we discovered Marriage Encounter and began to rebuild our relationship with the help of much better communication. Today there are some wonderful 'Engagement and Marriage' courses that have transformed so many Christian relationships (for example, the HTB Marriage Course, and *Time for Marriage*). Praise God for them!

Lord, we pray for those who are struggling in their marriages today, that your grace will heal and restore them.

ANN WARREN

Blessing the place where you live

Through the blessing of the upright the city is exalted, but by the mouth of the wicked it is destroyed. (NIV)

People who live holy and righteous lives make an enormous difference to the communities in which they live, providing a major resource for the good of others around them. They are the 'salt and light' that Jesus speaks of in the parables. Travelling round the country, I find it fascinating to see how often such people have transformed the society in which they live—though they themselves may be completely unaware of the difference that they are making.

In the 1946 film *It's a Wonderful Life*, James Stewart plays the character of George, who becomes so depressed that he wishes he had never been born. Unbeknown to him, his guardian angel sets in train a rerun of his past life, but this time without George playing any part in the story. As he returns home, George is horrified to discover that the brother he had saved from drowning is no longer there, and that, as a consequence, many hundreds of people whom his brother had later rescued on a troopship have also perished. His eccentric uncle has been shut up in an asylum, without George there to protect him, and the whole town has been taken over and exploited by a greedy property owner whom George opposed and defeated when he was a part of the community.

Of course, none of us ever get to hear about our lives in the past tense like this, or see the blessing we may have been to people around us, but perhaps we need to take these verses from Proverbs to heart and actively seek ways in which we can be more of a blessing to others.

Ask God to show you the difference your life has made to the people around you, and pray that this will encourage you to do even more in the days ahead.

ANN WARREN

Be kind to the poor

Whoever is kind to the poor lends to the Lord, and he will reward them for what they have done. (NIV)

Throughout the book of Proverbs, God's special love and concern for the poor is very evident. We sometimes pride ourselves on our welfare system in the UK, but many families, especially single parents, are struggling to cope on very low wages today. Although there is a benefits system in place, at the time of writing any change in circumstances will automatically terminate the existing payment, leaving something like a five-week gap with no money or food available for struggling families. Where previously we have often thought of the poor as surviving famine conditions in some distant corner of Africa, now there are plenty of needy people right here on our own doorstep.

Food banks round the country are now providing very welcome help and support to people in need and are a wonderful way for Christians to show that they care. The people who come to the one my church is involved in really appreciate what is being given, and often express a wish to help out as soon as they find themselves in a position to do so. Many comment on the fact that we work from a church and want to know more about the reason we are all giving our time in this way.

It can be very humiliating for people to admit that they need help to obtain food, so it is even more important to make them feel valued and loved. We always make time to sit with them and lend a listening ear. Help like this is so much more valuable than mere words and so much closer to the heart of God. When we offer help to the poor, it is as if we are giving directly to God, and he promises to pay back with interest.

Heavenly Father, please open my eyes to the need and suffering around me. Show me where and how I can expand my heart to look after those that you care about so deeply.

ANN WARREN

Pride comes before a fall

Do not exalt yourself in the king's presence, and do not claim a place among his great men; it is better for him to say to you, 'Come up here,' than for him to humiliate you before his nobles. (NIV)

One virtue that is very definitely not in fashion today is that of humility. Although it is obviously good for people to have confidence in the gifts they have been given, I sometimes find it really difficult when young people are encouraged to exaggerate when talking of their abilities or writing their CVs. Some reality TV shows, such as *The Apprentice* make a virtue out of such boastfulness.

Whether it is a tennis player talking about how well he played today, or someone claiming to have made a great success of a particular project on their CV, this amount of self-congratulation sometimes goes against the spirit of humility. There is surely a balance to be found here. By contrast, it is humbling when someone who genuinely has every reason to feel proud does not claim any kind of greatness or think of herself as anything special.

I will never forget the time when I moved house after being recently widowed and suffering with serious back problems. Two wonderful friends came in to help me and do all the things that I could not possibly have done myself. I couldn't help thinking how amazed people would have been to see one of them, a well-known minister, with his sleeves rolled up, carrying out the most menial of tasks to help me, without a single word of complaint.

To me, that is true humility, because however able, clever or well known we may be, we are called to humble service, to follow the example of our God who loves us and who would stoop to wash our feet.

Dear Lord, please help me not to think too highly of myself. May I remember that everything I have comes from you, and that without you I am nothing.

ANN WARREN

Never put off till tomorrow...

Go to the ant you sluggard; consider its ways and be wise! It has no commander, no overseer or ruler, yet it stores its provisions in summer and gathers its food at harvest. (NIV)

'Sluggard' is such an ugly, emotive word that I am sure none of us will recognise ourselves in it, yet the passage continues, 'A little sleep... a little folding of the hands to rest...'. I wonder if, like me, you just love those extra few minutes in bed, or if you too are given to procrastination. We can always find some valid-sounding excuse for not doing what needs to be done just at this very moment. The phrase 'I'll do it tomorrow' all too easily springs to mind.

One of the habits I had to develop while writing from home in my own time (as opposed to working from an office towards a radio or press deadline) was to set a time to write and make myself stick to it, regardless of all other interruptions. It was a very hard lesson to learn, but an incredibly valuable one. So often, people who are retired or looking after children or working from home find exactly the same problem—when and how to spend time alone with God or how to fit in that visit or phone call that we know needs to be made. But all of us need to learn to organise our time properly.

It is so much easier just to get the essential chores done and then find somewhere to crash and have some 'me' time. This is fine up to a point, but if we allow ourselves too much self-indulgence, the key relationships that make life really worthwhile—and, above all, our relationship with God—will suffer as a result. Perhaps we need to review how we use the precious time we've been given, which won't come again.

Heavenly Father, please help me to make time for the really important relationships in my life, such as my relationship with you, and show me how best to do it.

ANN WARREN

Choose your friends wisely

A friend loves at all times, and a brother is born for a time of adversity. (NIV)

My friends have been absolutely key to me down the years. Having been orphaned at an early age, with no brothers or sisters, I have depended on my friends through thick and thin. They are actually like my own well-chosen family.

Firstly, I know that I can trust each one of them, as they can trust me—and there is no price to put on such a relationship. The book of Proverbs tells us to steer clear of a long list of types of people—those with lying lips, anyone with haughty eyes (who perhaps think too highly of themselves), people who are quick to bear false witness, or those who rush to do evil.

These may sound quite extreme characteristics, but it can be a timely warning if we see a potential friend who seems likely to take advantage of others, who is quick to justify something we know to be wrong, or is perhaps just quick to spread gossip.

When we can love and trust our friends, we know that we can share anything with them, and that any secret will be safe with them. I can't imagine life without such friends, and we have shared many 'deep things of the heart' over the years.

This is particularly true in times of adversity. I have been completely overwhelmed in the past by the number of friends who have rallied round when we were in trouble and urgently needed prayer support. When my first husband was dying of cancer, a group of friends from the local church committed themselves to meeting with us regularly, to pray for us and for any needs we had at the time. Being surrounded by such wonderful friends completely transformed the suffering we were going through.

Ask God to show you the people you can really trust to befriend, and pray for some way that you could also be a blessing to them.

ANN WARREN

Give God the first and the best

Honour the Lord with your wealth, with the firstfruits of all your crops; then your barns will be filled to overflowing, and your vats will brim over with new wine. (NIV)

To some people, putting just a handful of change in the church collection plate seems more than enough, but for those of us who have discovered the amazing generosity of God, setting aside a tithe of what we earn will have become a key principle. We will also have discovered the amazing generosity of God in return.

Household names such as Cadbury and Bournville are wonderful examples of how, when the Quaker business owners gave not only to God but also to the welfare and proper housing of their own employees, God abundantly blessed them so that their 'barns' were indeed overflowing.

I always find it fascinating that the most generous people are those who know all about poverty and hardship themselves. Where I used to live, it was a well-known fact that collectors for Christian Aid would raise much more money from poorer housing areas than from those whose residents were distinctly well-heeled and could afford to give much more.

This is also true in some very poor countries where they understand what a privilege it is to be able to give to God's work, and where people often even ask to be allowed to give sacrificially. Anyone who has discovered for themselves the amazing generosity of God will know that he is no one's debtor.

We cannot all up sticks and leave home to run an aid project in the developing world or play an organising role in an anti-poverty drive—but we can all give sacrificially and become a vital part of God's work with our money and with our prayers.

Ask God to show you some way of giving, whether it is your time or your money, and watch how the blessings return to you.

ANN WARREN

The perfect wife

A wife of noble character who can find? She is worth far more than rubies. Her husband has confidence in her and lacks nothing of value. (NIV)

This picture of a perfect wife is nothing if not daunting, and few of us who are married are able to live up to it. Of course, it is very much a snapshot of its time—not many of us 'select wool and flax' and 'provide portions for our servant girls'—but we should not discount the values expressed in the passage.

For a start, her husband has full confidence in her and trusts her with everything. This is not the 'little woman at home' that earlier Christian teaching liked to emphasise; it is actually much more contemporary. She is a businesswoman in her own right: 'She considers a field and buys it; out of her earnings she plants a vineyard… She sees that her trading is profitable' (vv. 16, 18). There is no attempt to play down her ability here: 'She speaks with wisdom and faithful instruction is on her tongue' (v. 26).

The key to it all is, of course, that she 'fears the Lord' (v. 30), and this counts for more than her charm and beauty, which will inevitably fade. The Proverbs wife is deeply respected by all and is indeed a model for both married and unmarried women, then and today.

The Proverbs writers are at pains to emphasise how important the choice of a marriage partner is. As the marriage service puts it, it is not a state to be entered 'unadvisedly or lightly' but 'in the fear of God'. This choice will affect not only the couple's future happiness but the faith and security of any children entrusted to them.

Whether we are married or unmarried, walking 'in the fear of God', knowing our identity and dignity in him, is of the greatest importance.

Lord, please develop in me the 'noble character' that will bring glory to your name.

ANN WARREN

Jesus' high priestly prayer

Sandra Wheatley writes:

'Give ear to my words, O Lord, consider my meditation. Hearken to the voice of my cry, my King, and my God: for unto thee will I pray. My voice shalt thou hear in the morning, O Lord; in the morning will I direct my prayer unto thee, and will look up' (Psalm 5:1–3, KJV).

Of all the works we are called to, of all the gifts we are given, and of all the journeys we will ever make, I am convinced that there is no higher calling, no greater gift and no journey as exciting as the one we're called to when we embrace prayer. Like many people, I am exhilarated and mystified by prayer. Sometimes I think I understand what it is, and have within my grasp just the right 'way or words' to make a difference. Then I realise that I still have so much more to learn, such depths to plumb, as I seek an audience with my God each day.

The main focus of these notes will be Jesus' 'high priestly prayer' in John 17, as well as other examples of prayer in scripture. I'm sure there will be many familiar phrases that have been etched into our hearts and lives, but I hope and pray that we'll find some new treasures as we take time to draw alongside Jesus and learn from him.

If you have access to the internet, look up 'Psalm 5 Chuck Girard' on YouTube. I first heard this song version 45 years ago; then, as now, it formed the soundtrack to my days. As I listen to it again, the words evoke a lovely picture of Jesus looking up and praying, just as we do, and just as he taught us to do. How lovely is that! And how exciting to have the opportunity once again to sit at Jesus' feet and learn from him.

The Lord's Prayer

After Jesus said this, he looked towards heaven and prayed: 'Father, the hour has come. Glorify your Son, that your Son may glorify you.' (NIV)

So many fabulous and encouraging things have been written about Jesus' high priestly prayer that, for me, this *is* 'the Lord's Prayer'. It is only 647 words long and takes a few minutes to read, yet it is the longest recorded prayer of Jesus. It's full of emotion as well as devotion and is such a contrast to his prayer in Gethsemane—but this is the same Jesus praying to the same God and allowing his disciples, and us, to eavesdrop on the Father–Son relationship.

In the previous chapters of the Gospel, Jesus speaks from God to the disciples; now he is looking toward heaven and speaking to God for them. Isn't that wonderful? In essence, this prayer shows Jesus looking towards God, looking around as he prays for the disciples, and looking ahead as he prays for you and me.

As an example of where to begin as we pray, there can be no better way than looking towards God, knowing that our gaze meets his. At its simplest and most sublime, it is the shifting of our gaze, focusing away from our cares and worries and the things we can see, and on to the God whom we know.

Jesus, as he 'looked towards heaven', knew what lay ahead of him. He knew what heaven looked like; he knew what to expect; he knew he was going home. For us, all we can do is imagine what lies ahead as this life becomes the next life and we move on and into our eternal home. I can't wait!

If prayer is still a challenge and a struggle for you, I do hope that as we explore a little of Jesus' prayer in the coming days, we will embrace it in its simplest form and glean some gems from it.

Lord, there may be many distractions today that demand my time and attention, but in these brief moments help me to look away from what is around and look to you. Let me catch a glimpse of your gaze meeting mine.

SANDRA WHEATLEY

The value of one hour

'Father, the hour has come.' (NIV)

I cannot read this prayer without being gripped by the fact that Jesus knew he was facing the cross: this was 'the hour'. Of the 29,000 hours that Jesus had lived, this one was the reason for his birth and life—his death. The hour of our redeemer's death became the hour of redemption's birth.

How many hours had Jesus lived since the wedding in Cana, when he said to Mary, 'My hour has not yet come' (John 2:4)? How many hours had he prayed, travelled, healed and taught those around him? Jesus lived a full-on life, and all his hours were filled with significance.

A lot can happen in 60 minutes. How many situations have we faced that have changed radically in just 60 minutes? I've no way of knowing what you face today, no way of knowing what this particular 'hour' may hold for you. But I pray that it is a significant one.

Some years ago, I faced one of the hardest struggles I've known. I was going through the horrors of withdrawing from medication that had been prescribed for pain relief. It hadn't helped and was affecting me emotionally and psychologically—so much so that life had begun to feel futile.

I read Paul's words penned from his prison cell: 'I have kept the faith' (2 Timothy 4:7). Something sparked within me and I started to look at the clock each hour, whispering, 'I have kept the faith… I have kept the faith.' For weeks, and through sleepless, agonising nights, I would look at the clock, repeating, 'I have kept the faith' for one hour… then the next and the next. I came through! I had kept the faith—and the faith, and God, had kept me.

So much can happen today; there is so much potential in every moment of every hour we live. Let's make each one count for him.

Dear Lord, as moments become hours today, fill each one with your presence and let your love flow from my life to others. Amen

SANDRA WHEATLEY

This is it!

'Now this is eternal life: that they know you, the only true God, and Jesus Christ, whom you have sent.' (NIV)

I sometimes wonder if Jesus shouted out this verse. It contains the bedrock of what being a Christian is, and I wonder why it took me years to actually 'get it'.

When I accepted Jesus into my life, I thought 'eternal life' started when we step into eternity, as this life ends. At the time, it made sense to an eleven-year-old: if I carried on believing in Jesus, then one day I would have eternal life. I'd be dead… but hey… I'd really be 'alive'.

Then this priceless gem caught the light: 'Now…'. Not tomorrow, or years hence, but today. Not some future time, but my relationship with God through Jesus, now! Every moment of every day is an eternal-life moment. It has already begun, and seals what scripture says in Ecclesiastes 3:11: 'He has also set eternity in the human heart.' Jesus' prayer confirms this amazing truth.

Marcus Rainford writes, 'Natural life is his creation; spiritual life is his inspiration; eternal life is his gift' (*Thoughts on John 17*). I've seen that 'gift' of knowing God deeply worked out in my dad's life. Dad is 87 years old. When my mum died in 2011, the pain my dad felt was almost tangible. He begged God to take it away and to bring a sense of his presence that would ease the terrible loneliness. God answered his prayer, not by taking away the pain and loneliness totally, but by giving Dad a taste of his goodness and a glimpse of what he has in store for him, until the day he will see my mum again.

My dad knows God more deeply than he ever imagined. That is eternal life. I thank God for my dad and his example to me as he trusts his heavenly Father.

Lord, thank you for all our elderly parents. Help their children to cherish them and learn from them. Amen

SANDRA WHEATLEY

Going home

'And now, Father, glorify me in your presence with the glory I had with you before the world began.' (NIV)

As Jesus concludes this first part of his prayer, he looks forward to being in God's presence and recollects the glory he had 'before the world began'. There is a sense here of the utter humanness of Jesus. In order to cope with all that is about to happen to him—the agony of Gethsemane and the horrors of the cross—he recalls how things *were*, before anything *was*. Jesus laid aside the glory he had; he laid aside his majesty; he laid aside any immunity from pain and shame, so that his death could bring us life (Philippians 2:6–7).

His agony on the cross would be felt as a man, as well as God, so it makes sense that he, like us, needed to muster all the strength he could for what lay ahead. Jesus does that here. He is going home, into the presence of God and into the glory he had before anything existed, and at this point in his prayer it is almost as if he pauses, remembers, and gains the strength he needs from that memory.

There have been many times in my life when 'going home' has galvanised my failing strength and weary heart. I realise that, for some people, the idea of 'home' holds more dread than security, and home has been a place to leave without a backward glance. Yet for each of us who now know Jesus as our Lord and Saviour, he has promised us a home that we can look forward to, where we will be safe, where we will be known, cherished and loved.

There is something about Jesus' words that I really identify with. My 'homesick-for-heaven' heart finds a resonance with his as he looks forward to the glory he had and will soon return to, in the presence of God the Father.

Father God, when our days here are difficult, strengthen our hearts and remind us of the home we have with you in heaven. Amen

SANDRA WHEATLEY

Jesus' prayer for the disciples

'I have revealed you to those whom you gave me out of the world. They were yours; you gave them to me and they have obeyed your word.' (NIV)

As we move into the next part of Jesus' prayer, his gaze shifts from his relationship with his Father to his disciples. I wonder if he prayed with eyes open, looking at each one—Peter, John, James, Andrew, Phillip and the others. If he did, then these words take on an extra poignancy, as they were among the last words Jesus would say over them as a group. This section of the prayer is the longest: that's how important this group is to him. He loves these men (and women) who have been with him and witnessed so much and understood so little. Now the time is approaching when he will leave them. But he leaves such precious words with them: they are a farewell to Jesus' earthly ministry and, as such, hold huge significance.

One of the key words in these verses is 'giving': the word is used five times in verses 6–8. Notice how Jesus speaks of his disciples: they were the Father's, given to him out of the world, God's chosen gifts to his Son. As he prayed these words, I wonder if a light was beginning to dawn in the disciples' hearts. Theirs was no haphazard appointment; they had been chosen by God, given to his Son. Maybe Jesus wanted to remind them of that, to prepare them for the coming days when doubts and fears would crowd in and these precious moments would be dimmed.

Jesus also says that he has given the disciples the words that God gave to him. The words Jesus spoke would seal and secure the salvation the disciples received. There was to be no greater gift: Jesus had no possessions, no wealth to leave, just words from the Father's Word who became flesh.

Read John 1:1–2 and 14. Amen!

SANDRA WHEATLEY

Name above all names

'While I was with them, I protected them and kept them safe by that name you gave me... My prayer is not that you take them out of the world but that you protect them from the evil one.' (NIV)

I wonder how many times Jesus protected the disciples during his time with them. We know that he calmed the storm (Mark 6:45–53), but how many other times were their lives at risk as they followed him? They lived in turbulent and dangerous times.

Jesus had kept them safe—safe by the Name and by all that it means. There can be no safer place than 'in the shelter of the Most High' (Psalm 91:1), protected by everything the Name denotes—the character and the attributes of God Almighty himself.

Now Jesus asks that his Father continue that protection. In particular, he asks that they be protected from the evil one. Unbeknown to them, in a few hours they would be facing their greatest challenge and the greatest onslaught from the evil one. But they were safe: Jesus' prayer was answered.

Do you ever wonder how much easier our lives would be if, the moment we became Christians, we were whisked off home to heaven, avoiding all the nasty experiences of life and all the taunts and discouragements the evil one aims at us? Perhaps for us it would be better, but what about this watching, waiting, sin-soaked world? No, we are here for his purposes, here to know him and to make him known—to pass on what we have received from him so that the work entrusted to us can be completed and the world can know that Jesus is the Son of God.

Please read Ephesians 6:10–18. It reminds us of our battle and of his resources. We are armed and dangerous—in his name and by his strength!

Father God, thank you for your safekeeping and protection from the evil one, for me and for those I love, day by day.

SANDRA WHEATLEY

Jesus' prayer for us

'My prayer is not for them alone. I pray also for those who will believe in me through their message.' (NIV)

Again Jesus' prayer shifts a little. He now looks further, much further, ahead.

One of the first Bibles I received after coming to faith was a red-letter KJV. When I turned to John's Gospel, and chapters 14—17, my eyes widened at the pages full of red print denoting Jesus' own words. Then, as I found this verse, something burned in my spirit. Jesus said that he was praying for me! Down through the centuries, Jesus had seen me. He prayed for me on the night he was betrayed. For a rebellious, disruptive eleven-year-old who didn't feel as if she figured much in anyone's life, here were words of hope and comfort. Jesus knew me and had been praying for me through the centuries.

Jesus prayed (and is praying) for you, right now (Hebrews 7:25). Let's pause a moment to let that sink in.

One of the greatest comforts I have is knowing that friends are praying for me. Some years ago, I started a 'BCC' (blind copy) group in my email address book. I email everyone on it regularly with my prayer requests. The names are confidential and no one knows who else is on the list. They are precious friends from around the world. When I'm in distress, I email them; the moment I do, I sense a change in my circumstances as I know someone is praying for me alongside the God who always is.

We all need prayerful support. Many of you will be part of a prayer group or have joined other prayer initiatives, and you know what power there is in concerted prayer. Many of us will have come to faith because, years ago, someone began to pray for us—a relative, a friend or a minister. There is immense power in prayer to change people and situations.

Dear Lord, please be with anyone who is feeling isolated, in a situation where no one sees or can understand. Please assure them that you know and see and you're praying for them even now. Amen

SANDRA WHEATLEY

One body

'May they experience such perfect unity that the world will know that you sent me and that you love them as much as you love me.' (NLT)

Jesus prays for unity again—for the third time in this prayer. It was important to him; it still is. But why did he pray for unity rather than anything else that the disciples, and we, would undoubtedly need? Could it be that everything we seek to do or have received from God will be to no avail without unity?

Is Jesus speaking about church unity or the unity of believers? I'm not sure Jesus is praying for an ecumenical movement or that we will all join the same denomination, but rather that we as believers might live in unity with him, the Father and the Spirit, and with one another. One + One + One + one = *One*!

Nevertheless, when we're able to stand together as believers, the world takes notice. The scriptures give only one example of how the world will know that we love Jesus—by our love for one another (John 13:35). The church is called to unity and I am a huge advocate of working closely together across the denominational divide, despite our differences and diversities. The church was born in the heart of God and we are privileged to be 'living stones' (1 Peter 2:5), not clones.

Seeing Jesus pray with such passion for unity among us, a desire develops within me to be an answer to that prayer. There remains an immense potential in God's 'gathered people', his church. Despite the ecumenical differences and the doctrines that can divide us, the church was his idea and was built on the revelation that he is the Christ (Matthew 16:16–18). He entrusted it into our hands to make him known—by the way we love one another.

Here is another mystery: he calls such diverse, damaged people as you and me and somehow makes himself known through us, by the way we love one another.

Father God, may you be seen in the 'living stones' you have redeemed and fashioned to be your church. Amen

SANDRA WHEATLEY

To be with Jesus

'Father, I want those you have given me to be with me where I am.'
(NIV)

Many aspects of Jesus' prayer are like his last will and testament, but with one major difference: Jesus has no possessions to pass on, no assets, no riches. Yet what he does pass on, the things he asks the Father to grant, go way beyond any worldly riches.

The request Jesus makes is a gem! He asks that we may be with him, where he is. We have a place with him, a place he has prepared, a place where we will belong, where we will fit in (John 14:2)—the grandest of 'grand designs'.

For over 50 years Jesus has been in my life; he's been with me to many places. He is such a welcome companion, but the time will come when he takes me to his place. I cannot fathom what that will be like. I used to imagine 'heaven' as it's painted in the book of Revelation, but the day my mum died, the picture dimmed. I couldn't see her in heaven, as I still was coming to terms with this life without her. What I know for certain, though, is that Mum is with Jesus: she is where he is. One day he'll call me to be there too.

In one of my struggles to come to terms with disability, I recalled childhood days and, in particular, the chase around the houses where we lived as my mum tried to round us up after a long day of playing outside. I would go into our house through the front door, and run straight out again through the back door. Mum eventually caught me—not by chasing me but by waiting inside and then locking the doors.

When my 'playing-out' days were done and God was calling me to spend more time indoors with him, that memory flooded back. It was time to be with God—to stay, watch and pray.

Lord, one day we'll move from this life to the next, to the home you have been preparing for us. Then we'll see you as you see us, and know you as you know us. We will see your glory. Thank you.

SANDRA WHEATLEY

It will never end

'I have made you known to them and will continue to make you known.' (NIV)

The final verse of John 17 may be the end of Jesus' prayer, but there is no 'Amen'. Isn't that wonderful? Why? Because Jesus says that he will 'continue to make God known', and this is as true today as it was then (Romans 8:34; Hebrews 7:25).

There is so much more to this prayer than I've been able to express, but I hope that what I've written will encourage you to use Jesus' prayer as a template for your own, whether you join with others or pray alone. I hope that you might pray for yourself without feeling that it's a selfish thing to do, pray for others as you hear of their needs and concerns, and pray for those yet to come to faith—that the love you share with your fellow Christians may bear fruit.

Many excellent resources are available to encourage and to teach us about prayer. There are worldwide groups of women drawn together to pray, as well as those out-of-sight people whose prayers and intercessions are seen and heard by God alone. We can all pray.

I once heard prayer described as 'the breath of the soul'. Unless we have a serious respiratory problem, we rarely notice that we're breathing; our bodies just get on and do it. It is far harder to hold our breath than it is to breathe. Just as our lungs are the organs of respiration, so prayer is the breath of the soul, the 'organ' by which we receive him into our parched and weary hearts. This gives a whole new meaning to the instruction to 'pray continually' (1 Thessalonians 5:17). Every breath is a prayer.

Nowadays I have the luxury of time, and I choose to invest in the privilege of prayer, in whatever shape or form it takes—quiet adoration, supplication, intercession or silence.

Father God, at any given moment, we are granted an audience with you, the King of glory—all because of this gift of prayer. Thank you, Lord.

SANDRA WHEATLEY

Still learning and growing

'One day Jesus was praying in a certain place. When he finished, one of his disciples said to him, 'Lord, teach us to pray.' (NIV)

This heartfelt plea still resonates with me. I am still learning what it is to pray as Jesus did.

Prayer has the capacity to thrill or daunt us. We can hassle ourselves into a frenzy sometimes if we feel our words aren't 'right' or if we feel so wretched about ourselves that our prayers seem to hit the ceiling and bounce back. Why would the divine 'bend low and hear my whispered plea' (Psalm 31:2, LB)? The mystery is that he does. There is something so simple about prayer that we often miss it, or we feel the need to dress it up and make it into something it isn't. In answer to the disciples' plea, Jesus gave them and us the Lord's Prayer—simple and sublime.

Someone has said that prayer is for the helpless—and it is. Numbers 21:4–9 gives a wonderful illustration of our helplessness: when the Israelites were dying from snake bites, God told Moses to erect a brass snake and said that the people only needed to look up at it to be healed. Jesus reminds his followers of this story in John 3:14–15. He too will be 'lifted up', and anyone who believes—who looks up to him—will be saved.

When 'disability' replaced ability in my life and I needed to relinquish much of what I had held dear, I felt increasingly 'confined'. Even now, many of my days are spent staying put on my bed. But confinement doesn't mean restriction; if the rest of my body is hampered and disabled because of MS, my spirit and soul can still soar 'on wings like eagles'—and if I am unable to move any other part of my body because of the MS, I can still lift my eyes to him in prayer.

Read Psalm 121 as a prayer—your prayer for today.

SANDRA WHEATLEY

It's our turn now

They all joined together constantly in prayer, along with the women and Mary the mother of Jesus, and with his brothers. (NIV)

After Jesus' ascension, the disciples returned to Jerusalem. Despite the immense danger they were in, they remained together and they prayed. This is the first mention of the disciples praying together. They followed the example of Jesus, and the early church was founded on prayer. We follow on, praying continually that his kingdom may come.

While writing these notes, I've looked at many other examples in scripture of people who prayed—among them Abraham, Jacob, Hannah, David, Solomon, Jonah, Job, Daniel, Mary, Elizabeth, Peter and Paul. There are apparently 176 prayers in the Old Testament and 46 in the New Testament. So when we pray, we're in very good company.

If you have some time to spare, take a little tour through the scriptures and be encouraged by the prayers of the saints. They were just like you and me: they struggled and felt dismayed and discouraged, and yet they prayed—and God answered.

It's my prayer, in concluding this short series, that you too will continue to revel in your prayer life. If, like mine, it stutters every now and then, just remember the simplicity of prayer. It's a conversation, not a monologue, and often it is just 'being' with God.

Jesus ended his high priestly prayer: 'I have made you known to them, and will continue to make you known in order that the love you have for me may be in them and that I myself may be in them' (John 17:26). If we make that our starting-point as we pray, it will ensure that our prayers are fuelled by love and inspired by the Holy Spirit. Whatever shape they take—intercessions, supplications or adoration—we meet with God as we pray. And as we make him known, living among those yet to come to faith, we become part of God's answer to Jesus' prayer. How wonderful is that?

Lord, please teach me to pray. Amen

SANDRA WHEATLEY

Recommended reading

Combining missional vision with practical advice, these resources, written by Laura Treneer, give you the tools you need to transform your church communications. Ideal for church teams who want to reach their communities effectively, and a perfect gift for church leaders and volunteers who are short on time but need fast relevant advice.

Church Online: Websites
978 0 85746 552 8 £3.99

Church Online: Social media
978 0 85746 557 3 £3.99

Church from the Outside
978 0 85746 553 5 £3.99

Church from the Inside
978 0 85746 554 2 £3.99

brfonline.org.uk

God's Belongers should transform our thinking about what it means to belong to church. David Walker offers a fourfold model of belonging: through relationship, through place, through events, and through activities. He shows how 'belonging' can encompass a far wider group of people than those who attend weekly services, opening up creative opportunities for mission in today's world.

God's Belongers
How people engage with God today and how the church can help
David Walker
978 0 85746 467 5 £8.99
brfonline.org.uk

To order

Online: **brfonline.org.uk**
Tel.: +44 (0)1865 319700
Mon–Fri 9.15–17.30

Delivery times within the UK are normally
15 working days. Prices are correct at the time of
going to press but may change without prior notice.

Title	Price	Qty	Total
Church Online: Websites	£3.99		
Church Online: Social media	£3.99		
Church from the Outside: Displays, noticeboards, invitations, PR	£3.99		
Church from the Inside: Welcome, news sheets, magazines, stories	£3.99		
God's Belongers	£8.99		

POSTAGE AND PACKING CHARGES			
Order value	UK	Europe	Rest of world
Under £7.00	£1.25	£3.00	£5.50
£7.00–£29.99	£2.25	£5.50	£10.00
£30.00 and over	FREE	Prices on request	

Total value of books	
Postage and packing	
Total for this order	

Please complete in BLOCK CAPITALS

Title .... First name/initials .... Surname...

Address..

....Postcode ....

Acc. No. .... Telephone ....

Email..

Please keep me informed about BRF's books and resources ❏ by email ❏ by post
Please keep me informed about the wider work of BRF ❏ by email ❏ by post

Method of payment

❏ Cheque (made payable to BRF) ❏ MasterCard / Visa

Card no. ☐☐☐☐ ☐☐☐☐ ☐☐☐☐ ☐☐☐☐ ☐☐☐☐

Valid from M M Y Y Expires M M Y Y Security code* ☐☐☐
Last 3 digits on the reverse of the card

Signature* .... Date .... / .... / ....
*ESSENTIAL IN ORDER TO PROCESS YOUR ORDER

Please return this form with the appropriate payment to:

BRF, 15 The Chambers, Vineyard, Abingdon OX14 3FE | enquiries@brf.org.uk
To read our terms and find out about cancelling your order, please visit brfonline.org.uk/terms.

SUBSCRIPTION INFORMATION

Each issue of *Day by Day with God* is available from Christian bookshops everywhere. Copies may also be available through your church book agent or from the person who distributes Bible reading notes in your church.

Alternatively you may obtain *Day by Day with God* on subscription direct from the publishers. There are two kinds of subscription:

Individual subscriptions
covering 3 issues for 4 copies or less, payable in advance
(including postage & packing).

To order, please complete the details on page 144 and return with the appropriate payment to: BRF, 15 The Chambers, Vineyard, Abingdon OX14 3FE

You can also use the form on page 144 to order a gift subscription for a friend.

Group subscriptions
covering 3 issues for 5 copies or more, sent to **one** UK address (post free).

Please note that the annual billing period for group subscriptions runs from 1 May to 30 April.

To order, please complete the details on page 143 and return with the appropriate payment to: BRF, 15 The Chambers, Vineyard, Abingdon OX14 3FE

You will receive an invoice with the first issue of notes.

All our Bible reading notes can be ordered online by visiting
biblereadingnotes.org.uk/subscriptions

For information about our other Bible reading notes,
and apps for iPhone and iPod touch, visit
biblereadingnotes.org.uk

All subscription enquiries should be directed to:
BRF, 15 The Chambers, Vineyard, Abingdon OX14 3FE
+44 (0)1865 319700 | enquiries@brf.org.uk

DAY BY DAY WITH GOD GROUP SUBSCRIPTION FORM

All our Bible reading notes can be ordered online by visiting
biblereadingnotes.org.uk/subscriptions

The group subscription rate for *Day by Day with God* will be £13.20 per person until April 2018.

☐ I would like to take out a group subscription for .... (quantity) copies.

☐ Please start my order with the September 2017 / January 2018 / May 2018* issue.
I would like to pay annually/receive an invoice* with each edition of the notes.
(*delete as appropriate)

Please do not send any money with your order. Send your order to BRF and we will send you an invoice. The group subscription year is from 1 May to 30 April. If you start subscribing in the middle of a subscription year we will invoice you for the remaining number of issues left in that year.

Name and address of the person organising the group subscription:

Title .... First name/initials .... Surname ....

Address ....

.... Postcode ....

Telephone .... Email ....

Church ....

Name of Minister ....

Name and address of the person paying the invoice if the invoice needs to be sent directly to them:

Title .... First name/initials .... Surname ....

Address ....

.... Postcode ....

Telephone .... Email ....

Please return this form with the appropriate payment to:
BRF, 15 The Chambers, Vineyard, Abingdon OX14 3FE

To read our terms and find out about cancelling your order, please visit **brfonline.org.uk/terms**.

The Bible Reading Fellowship is a Registered Charity (233280)

DAY BY DAY WITH GOD INDIVIDUAL/GIFT SUBSCRIPTION FORM

> To order online, please visit **biblereadingnotes.org.uk/subscriptions**

☐ I would like to give a gift subscription (please provide both names and addresses)
☐ I would like to take out a subscription myself (complete your name and address details only once)

Title .... First name/initials .... Surname ....

Address ....

.... Postcode ....

Telephone .... Email ....

Gift subscription name ....

Gift subscription address ....

.... Postcode ....

Gift message (20 words max. or include your own gift card):

....

....

Please send *Day by Day with God* beginning with the September 2017 / January 2018 / May 2018 issue (*delete as appropriate*):

(*please tick box*)

	UK	Europe	Rest of world
Day by Day with God	☐ £16.50	☐ £24.60	☐ £28.50
2-year subscription	☐ £30.00	N/A	N/A

Total enclosed £ .... (cheques should be made payable to 'BRF')

Please charge my MasterCard / Visa ☐ Debit card ☐ with £ ....

Card no. ☐☐☐☐ ☐☐☐☐ ☐☐☐☐ ☐☐☐☐

Valid from ☐M ☐M ☐Y ☐Y Expires ☐M ☐M ☐Y ☐Y Security code* ☐☐☐

Last 3 digits on the reverse of the card

Signature* .... Date ...... / ...... / ......

*ESSENTIAL IN ORDER TO PROCESS YOUR ORDER

Please return this form with the appropriate payment to:
BRF, 15 The Chambers, Vineyard, Abingdon OX14 3FE

To read our terms and find out about cancelling your order, please visit **brfonline.org.uk/terms**.

The Bible Reading Fellowship is a Registered Charity (233280)

DBDWG0217